Wonderful ways to prepare
DESSERTS

by JO ANN SHIRLEY

OTHER TITLES IN THIS SERIES

Printed in Canada.

Wonderful ways to prepare

DESSERTS

PLAYMORE INC NEW YORK USA
UNDER ARRANGEMENT WITH
I. WALDMAN & SON INC

**AYERS & JAMES PTY LTD
CROWS NEST AUSTRALIA**

**STAFFORD PEMBERTON PUBLISHING
KNUTSFORD UNITED KINGDOM**

FIRST PUBLISHED 1978

PUBLISHED IN THE USA
BY PLAYMORE INC.
UNDER ARRANGEMENT WITH I. WALDMAN & SON INC.

PUBLISHED IN AUSTRALIA
BY AYERS & JAMES PTY. LTD.
CROWS NEST.   AUSTRALIA

PUBLISHED IN THE UNITED KINGDOM
BY STAFFORD PEMBERTON PUBLISHING
KNUTSFORD CHESIRE

COPYRIGHT © 1978
AYERS & JAMES PTY. LTD.
5 ALEXANDER STREET
CROWS NEST   N.S.W.   AUSTRALIA

ISBN 0 86908 060 1

OVEN TEMPERATURE GUIDE

Description	Gas		Electric		Mark
	C	F	C	F	
Cool	100	200	110	225	¼
Very Slow	120	250	120	250	½
Slow	150	300	150	300	1-2
Moderately slow	160	325	170	340	3
Moderate	180	350	200	400	4
Moderately hot	190	375	220	425	5-6
Hot	200	400	230	450	6-7
Very hot	230	450	250	475	8-9

LIQUID MEASURES

IMPERIAL	METRIC
1 teaspoon	5 ml
1 tablespoon	20 ml
2 fluid ounces (¼ cup)	62.5 ml
4 fluid ounces (½ cup)	125 ml
8 fluid ounces (1 cup)	250 ml
1 pint (16 ounces — 2 cups)*	500 ml
* (The imperial pint is equal to 20 fluid ounces.)	

SOLID MEASURES

AVOIRDUPOIS	METRIC
1 ounce	30 g
4 ounces (¼ lb)	125 g
8 ounces (½ lb)	250 g
12 ounces (¾ lb)	375 g
16 ounces (1 lb)	500 g
24 ounces (1½ lb)	750 g
32 ounces (2 lb)	1000 g (1 kg)

CUP AND SPOON REPLACEMENTS FOR OUNCES

INGREDIENT	½ oz	1 oz	2 oz	3 oz	4 oz	5 oz	6 oz	7 oz	8 oz
Almonds, ground	2 T	¼ C	½ C	¾ C	1¼ C	1⅓ C	1⅔ C	2 C	2¼ C
slivered	6 t	¼ C	½ C	¾ C	1 C	1⅓ C	1⅔ C	2 C	2¼ C
whole	2 T	¼ C	⅓ C	½ C	¾ C	1 C	1¼ C	1⅓ C	1½ C
Apples, dried whole	3 T	½ C	1 C	1⅓ C	2 C	2⅓ C	2¾ C	3⅓ C	3¾ C
Apricots, chopped	2 T	¼ C	½ C	¾ C	1 C	1¼ C	1½ C	1¾ C	2 C
whole	2 T	3 T	½ C	⅔ C	1 C	1¼ C	1⅓ C	1½ C	1¾ C
Arrowroot	1 T	2 T	⅓ C	½ C	⅔ C	¾ C	1 C	1¼ C	1⅓ C
Baking Powder	1 T	2 T	⅓ C	½ C	⅔ C	¾ C	1 C	1 C	1¼ C
Baking Soda	1 T	2 T	⅓ C	½ C	⅔ C	¾ C	1 C	1 C	1¼ C
Barley	1 T	2 T	¼ C	½ C	⅔ C	¾ C	1 C	1 C	1¼ C
Breadcrumbs, dry	2 T	¼ C	½ C	¾ C	1 C	1¼ C	1½ C	1¾ C	2 C
soft	¼ C	½ C	1 C	1½ C	2 C	2½ C	3 C	3⅔ C	4¼ C
Biscuit Crumbs	2 T	¼ C	½ C	¾ C	1¼ C	1⅓ C	1⅔ C	2 C	2¼ C
Butter	3 t	6 t	¼ C	⅓ C	½ C	⅔ C	¾ C	1 C	1 C
Cheese, grated, lightly packed,									
natural cheddar	6 t	¼ C	½ C	¾ C	1 C	1¼ C	1½ C	1¾ C	2 C
Processed cheddar	5 t	2 T	⅓ C	⅔ C	¾ C	1 C	1¼ C	1½ C	1⅔ C
Parmesan, Romano	6 t	¼ C	½ C	¾ C	1 C	1⅓ C	1⅔ C	2 C	2¼ C
Cherries, candied, chopped	1 T	2 T	⅓ C	½ C	¾ C	1 C	1 C	1⅓ C	1½ C
whole	1 T	2 T	⅓ C	½ C	⅔ C	¾ C	1 C	1¼ C	1⅓ C
Cocoa	2 T	¼ C	½ C	¾ C	1¼ C	1⅓ C	1⅔ C	2 C	2¼ C
Coconut, desiccated	2 T	⅓ C	⅔ C	1 C	1⅓ C	1⅔ C	2 C	2⅓ C	2⅔ C
shredded	⅓ C	⅔ C	1¼ C	1¾ C	2½ C	3 C	3⅔ C	4⅓ C	5 C
Cornstarch	6 t	3 T	½ C	⅔ C	1 C	1¼ C	1½ C	1⅔ C	2 C
Corn Syrup	2 t	1 T	2 T	¼ C	⅓ C	½ C	½ C	⅔ C	⅔ C
Coffee, ground	2 T	⅓ C	⅔ C	1 C	1⅓ C	1⅔ C	2 C	2⅓ C	2⅔ C
instant	3 T	½ C	1 C	1⅓ C	1¾ C	2¼ C	2⅔ C	3 C	3½ C
Cornflakes	½ C	1 C	2 C	3 C	4¼ C	5¼ C	6¼ C	7⅓ C	8⅓ C
Cream of Tartar	1 T	2 T	⅓ C	½ C	⅔ C	¾ C	1 C	1 C	1¼ C
Currants	1 T	2 T	⅓ C	⅔ C	¾ C	1 C	1¼ C	1½ C	1⅔ C
Custard Powder	6 t	3 T	½ C	⅔ C	1 C	1¼ C	1½ C	1⅔ C	2 C
Dates, chopped	1 T	2 T	⅓ C	⅔ C	¾ C	1 C	1¼ C	1½ C	1⅔ C
whole, pitted	1 T	2 T	⅓ C	½ C	¾ C	1 C	1¼ C	1⅓ C	1½ C
Figs, chopped	1 T	2 T	⅓ C	½ C	¾ C	1 C	1 C	1⅓ C	1½ C
Flour, all-purpose or cake	6 t	¼ C	½ C	¾ C	1 C	1¼ C	1½ C	1¾ C	2 C
wholemeal	6 t	3 T	½ C	⅔ C	1 C	1¼ C	1⅓ C	1⅔ C	1¾ C
Fruit, mixed	1 T	2 T	⅓ C	½ C	¾ C	1 C	1¼ C	1⅓ C	1½ C
Gelatine	5 t	2 T	⅓ C	½ C	¾ C	1 C	1 C	1¼ C	1½ C
Ginger, crystallised pieces	1 T	2 T	⅓ C	½ C	¾ C	1 C	1¼ C	1⅓ C	1½ C
ground	6 t	⅓ C	½ C	¾ C	1¼ C	1½ C	1¾ C	2 C	2¼ C
preserved, heavy syrup	1 T	2 T	⅓ C	½ C	⅔ C	¾ C	1 C	1 C	1¼ C
Glucose, liquid	2 t	1 T	2 T	¼ C	⅓ C	½ C	½ C	⅔ C	⅔ C
Haricot Beans	1 T	2 T	⅓ C	½ C	⅔ C	¾ C	1 C	1 C	1¼ C

In this table, t represents teaspoonful, T represents tablespoonful and C represents cupful.

CUP AND SPOON REPLACEMENTS FOR OUNCES (Cont.)

INGREDIENT	½ oz	1 oz	2 oz	3 oz	4 oz	5 oz	6 oz	7 oz	8 oz
Honey	2 t	1 T	2 T	¼ C	⅓ C	½ C	½ C	⅔ C	⅔ C
Jam	2 t	1 T	2 T	¼ C	⅓ C	½ C	½ C	⅔ C	¾ C
Lentils	1 T	2 T	⅓ C	½ C	⅔ C	¾ C	1 C	1 C	1¼ C
Macaroni (see pasta)									
Milk Powder, full cream	2 T	¼ C	½ C	¾ C	1¼ C	1⅓ C	1⅔ C	2 C	2¼ C
non fat	2 T	⅓ C	¾ C	1¼ C	1½ C	2 C	2⅓ C	2¾ C	3¼ C
Nutmeg	6 t	3 T	½ C	⅔ C	¾ C	1 C	1¼ C	1½ C	1⅔ C
Nuts, chopped	6 t	¼ C	½ C	¾ C	1 C	1¼ C	1½ C	1¾ C	2 C
Oatmeal	1 T	2 T	½ C	⅔ C	¾ C	1 C	1¼ C	1½ C	1⅔ C
Olives, whole	1 T	2 T	⅓ C	⅔ C	¾ C	1 C	1¼ C	1½ C	1⅔ C
sliced	1 T	2 T	⅓ C	⅔ C	¾ C	1 C	1¼ C	1½ C	1⅔ C
Pasta, short (e.g. macaroni)	1 T	2 T	⅓ C	⅔ C	¾ C	1 C	1¼ C	1½ C	1⅔ C
Peaches, dried & whole	1 T	2 T	⅓ C	⅔ C	¾ C	1 C	1¼ C	1½ C	1⅔ C
chopped	6 t	¼ C	½ C	¾ C	1 C	1¼ C	1½ C	1¾ C	2 C
Peanuts, shelled, raw, whole	1 T	2 T	⅓ C	½ C	¾ C	1 C	1¼ C	1⅓ C	1½ C
roasted	1 T	2 T	⅓ C	⅔ C	¾ C	1 C	1¼ C	1½ C	1⅔ C
Peanut Butter	3 t	6 t	3 T	⅓ C	½ C	½ C	⅔ C	¾ C	1 C
Peas, split	1 T	2 T	⅓ C	½ C	⅔ C	¾ C	1 C	1 C	1¼ C
Peel, mixed	1 T	2 T	⅓ C	½ C	¾ C	1 C	1 C	1¼ C	1½ C
Potato, powder	1 T	2 T	¼ C	⅓ C	½ C	⅔ C	¾ C	1 C	1¼ C
flakes	¼ C	½ C	1 C	1⅓ C	2 C	2⅓ C	2¾ C	3⅓ C	3¾ C
Prunes, chopped	1 T	2 T	⅓ C	½ C	⅔ C	¾ C	1 C	1¼ C	1⅓ C
whole pitted	1 T	2 T	⅓ C	½ C	⅔ C	¾ C	1 C	1 C	1¼ C
Raisins	2 T	¼ C	⅓ C	½ C	¾ C	1 C	1 C	1⅓ C	1½ C
Rice, short grain, raw	1 T	2 T	¼ C	½ C	⅔ C	¾ C	1 C	1 C	1¼ C
long grain, raw	1 T	2 T	⅓ C	½ C	¾ C	1 C	1¼ C	1⅓ C	1½ C
Rice Bubbles	⅔ C	1¼ C	2½ C	3⅔ C	5 C	6¼ C	7½ C	8¾ C	10 C
Rolled Oats	2 T	⅓ C	⅔ C	1 C	1⅓ C	1¾ C	2 C	2½ C	2¾ C
Sago	2 T	¼ C	⅓ C	½ C	¾ C	1 C	1 C	1¼ C	1½ C
Salt, common	3 t	6 t	¼ C	⅓ C	½ C	⅔ C	¾ C	1 C	1 C
Semolina	1 T	2 T	⅓ C	½ C	¾ C	1 C	1 C	1⅓ C	1½ C
Spices	6 t	3 T	¼ C	⅓ C	½ C	½ C	⅔ C	¾ C	1 C
Sugar, plain	3 t	6 t	¼ C	⅓ C	½ C	⅔ C	¾ C	1 C	1 C
confectioners'	1 T	2 T	⅓ C	½ C	¾ C	1 C	1 C	1¼ C	1½ C
moist brown	1 T	2 T	⅓ C	½ C	¾ C	1 C	1 C	1⅓ C	1½ C
Tapioca	1 T	2 T	⅓ C	½ C	⅔ C	¾ C	1 C	1¼ C	1⅓ C
Treacle	2 t	1 T	2 T	¼ C	⅓ C	½ C	½ C	⅔ C	⅔ C
Walnuts, chopped	2 T	¼ C	½ C	¾ C	1 C	1¼ C	1½ C	1¾ C	2 C
halved	2 T	⅓ C	⅔ C	1 C	1¼ C	1½ C	1¾ C	2¼ C	2½ C
Yeast, dried	6 t	3 T	½ C	⅔ C	1 C	1¼ C	1⅓ C	1⅔ C	1¾ C
compressed	3 t	6 t	3 T	⅓ C	½ C	½ C	⅔ C	¾ C	1 C

In this table, t represents teaspoonful, T represents tablespoonful and C represents cupful.

Desserts

Boston Cream Cake

4 eggs, separated
1 cup sugar
4 tablespoons hot water
1 cup flour
1 teaspoon baking powder
⅛ teaspoon salt
1 teaspoon vanilla

Custard filling:
3 egg yolks
2 tablespoons flour
1 tablespoon cornstarch
½ cup confectioners' sugar
2 cups (500 ml) milk
2 tablespoons (40 g) butter
   or margarine

1. Beat egg yolks and sugar until thick and light yellow colored. Add water and sifted dry ingredients. Stir in vanilla.
2. Beat egg whites until stiff. Fold into mixture.
3. Butter and flour two 8-inch (20 cm) cake tins. Pour in cake mixture and bake in a 350°F (180°C) oven for twenty minutes. Cool.
4. In the top of a double boiler, mix together the egg yolks, flour, cornstarch, sugar, milk and butter or margarine. Place over simmering water and cook, stirring constantly, until mixture is thick and smooth. Cool.
5. Spread custard between the two layers and sprinkle confectioners' sugar on top.

Serves 6-8.

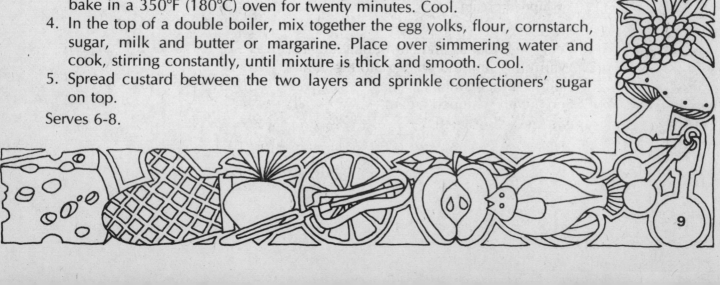

Raisin Cream Pie

Pastry:
2 cups flour
pinch of salt
½ cup (125 g) butter
   or margarine
cold water

Filling:
1 cup brown sugar
3 egg yolks, beaten
1 tablespoon (20 g) melted
   butter

1 cup raisins, cooked in
   a little water and drained
1 cup (120 g) coarsely
   chopped walnuts
pinch of salt
½ teaspoon cinnamon
¼ teaspoon nutmeg
3 egg yolks, stiffly
   beaten
1 teaspoon vanilla

1. Sift flour and salt into a mixing bowl. Rub in the butter or margarine with your fingertips until the mixture is like fine bread crumbs. Add enough cold water to form a stiff dough. Roll out half the dough to a thickness of ⅛ inch (3 mm) and line the bottom of 9-inch (23 cm) pie tin.
2. Combine brown sugar, egg yolks and butter. Add raisins, nuts, salt, cinnamon and nutmeg and mix thoroughly. Fold in egg whites and add vanilla.
3. Pour into the uncooked pastry shell.
4. Roll out other half of dough to a thickness of ⅛ inch (3 mm). Cut into strips and make a lattice top crust. Press edges together.
5. Bake in a 450°F (230°C) oven for ten minutes. Reduce heat to 350°F (180°C) and cook for another 20 minutes.

Serves 6-8.

Banana Madeleines

6 bananas
3 tablespoons raspberry jam
2 tablespoons desiccated
   coconut
whipped cream

1. Peel the bananas and cut in half lengthwise.
2. Warm the jam and brush onto the bananas.
3. Roll in the coconut.
4. Serve with whipped cream.

Serves 6.

Rich Cherry Torte

1 cup (250 g) butter
  or margarine
4 tablespoons sugar
½ teaspoon salt
2½ cups flour
1¼ teaspoons baking powder
2 cups cherries, pitted
½ cup (60 g) chopped blanched
  almonds

Custard:
3 teaspoons cornstarch
5 tablespoons sugar
pinch of salt

1 cup (250 ml) milk
5 egg yolks, slightly beaten
2 teaspoons vanilla

Meringue:
5 egg whites
5 tablespoons sugar
½ teaspoon baking powder
pinch of salt

1. Cream butter and sugar and add sifted dry ingredients. Press firmly on bottom and sides of a well-buttered spring form pan. Bake for fifteen minutes in a 425°F (220°C) oven.
2. To make custard, mix cornstarch, sugar and salt in the top of a double boiler. Add milk, then the egg yolks and place over simmering water. Cook, stirring constantly, until smooth and thick. Add vanilla and mix well.
3. Pour half the custard into the baked pie shell. Put cherries on top of the custard and then pour the remaining custard over the cherries.
4. Beat egg whites until stiff. Beat in sugar mixed with baking powder and salt. Spread on top of torte and sprinkle with chopped almonds. Bake in a 325°F (160°C) until meringue is brown.

Serves 8.

Frosted Grapes

1 lb (500 g) grapes
2 egg whites,
  slightly beaten
sugar

1. Dip clusters of grapes in egg whites. Set aside to dry.
2. When nearly dry, sprinkle with sugar.

Serves 6.

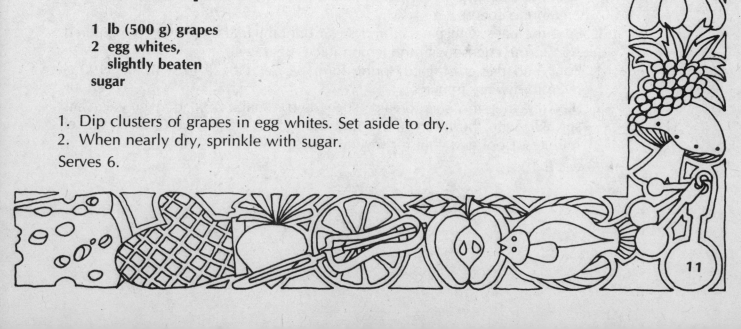

Banana Snow

6 bananas
2 tablespoons sugar
2 teaspoons lemon juice
1 cup plain yoghurt
1 cup (250 ml) cream
3 egg whites, stiffly beaten
chopped nuts

1. Peel and mash the bananas. Mix in sugar and lemon juice.
2. Add the yoghurt and cream and blend well.
3. Fold in egg whites and spoon into individual dishes. Sprinkle with chopped nuts.

Serves 6.

Cream Cheese Cake

Crust:
¾ lb (375 g) sweet plain cookies
   or graham crackers, crushed
¼ cup sugar
½ cup (125 g) butter
   or margarine, melted
2 teaspoons cinnamon

Filling:
1½ lb (750 g) cream cheese

⅛ teaspoon salt
1 cup sugar
4 eggs, well beaten
1 tablespoon lemon juice
2 cups (500 g) sour cream
⅓ cup sugar
1 teaspoon vanilla

1. To make the crust, combine all the ingredients and firmly press on sides and bottom of a 10-inch (25 cm) spring form pan. (Reserve about ½ cup of crumbs to sprinkle on top of cake.)
2. Cream the cheese.
3. Beat the eggs with the salt and sugar until thick and light yellow colored. Add to the cheese with the lemon juice. Beat well.
4. Pour into the crust-lined spring form pan and bake in a 375°F (190°C) oven for twenty minutes.
5. Mix together the sour cream, sugar and vanilla. Spread over cake and sprinkle with the reserved crumbs. Bake in a 475°F (250°C) oven for ten minutes. Cool and chill for several hours.

Serves 8-10.

Peach Cobbler

3 cups sliced fresh
   peaches
¾ cup sugar
3 tablespoons flour
2 tablespoons lemon juice
2 tablespoons (40 g) butter

½ teaspoon salt
4 teaspoons baking powder
1 tablespoon sugar
⅓ cup (83 g) butter
1 egg, well beaten
¾ cup (186 ml) milk

Topping:
2 cups flour

1. Put peaches in a greased baking dish.
2. Mix together sugar and flour. Sprinkle over the peaches. Sprinkle the lemon juice and then dot with butter.
3. For topping, sift dry ingredients and mix in butter until mixture is like coarse crumbs. Add combined egg and milk and mix until just moistened.
4. Drop dough in mounds over the peaches.
5. Bake in a 425°F (220°C) oven for 30 minutes.

Serves 8.

Almond Pudding

1 tablespoon gelatin
¼ cup cold water
½ cup hot water
½ cup sugar,
   caramelized
1 cup (250 ml) hot milk

1 cup (250 ml) cream,
   whipped
½ cup (57 g) toasted slivered
   almonds
½ teaspoon vanilla

1. Soak gelatin in cold water for five minutes. Dissolve in hot water.
2. Mix caramelized sugar and hot milk. Add to gelatin mixture and chill until partially set. Beat until frothy.
3. Fold in whipped cream, almonds and vanilla. Chill.

Serves 6.

Apple Crumble

1½ lb (750 g) cooking apples	½ cup (125 g) butter or margarine
⅓ cup (83 ml) water	1¼ cups flour
¾ cup brown sugar	½ cup sugar
2 teaspoons grated lemon rind	¼ teaspoon ginger
	½ teaspoon cinnamon

1. Peel, core and slice the apples.
2. Combine the water, sugar and lemon rind in a saucepan. Add the apple slices and cook, covered, until soft. Put into a well-buttered pie tin.
3. Combine butter or margarine, flour, sugar, ginger and cinnamon. Mix until mixture looks like fine bread crumbs. Sprinkle over the apples.
4. Bake in a 350°F (180°C) oven for about ½ hour or until golden brown. Serve warm.

Serves 4-6.

Honey Fruit Yoghurt

1 lb (500 g) cooking apples
2 tablespoons sugar
½ cup (125 ml) water
4 tablespoons honey
1½ cups (375 ml) plain yoghurt
3 tablespoons raisins

1. Peel, core and slice the apples. Put in a saucepan with the water and sugar and cook, covered, until soft. Cool. Drain.
2. Mix the honey with the yoghurt.
3. When the apples are cool, mix in the raisins. Place in individual dishes and top with the yoghurt and honey mixture.

Serves 4-6.

Coffee Pie

Pastry:
1 cup flour
pinch of salt
¼ cup (62.5 g) butter
   or margarine
cold water

Filling:
1 cup (250 ml) evaporated milk
½ cup (125 ml) very strong
   coffee
3 egg yolks, beaten

½ cup sugar
⅛ teaspoon salt
¼ teaspoon nutmeg
¼ teaspoon cinnamon
1 tablespoon gelatin
¼ cup (62.5 ml) cold water
1 teaspoon vanilla
3 egg whites, stiffly beaten
1 cup (250 ml) cream, whipped
3 tablespoons grated
   semi-sweet chocolate

1. Sift flour and salt into a mixing bowl. Rub in butter or margarine with your fingertips until the mixture looks like fine bread crumbs. Add enough water to form a stiff dough. Roll out to a thickness of ⅛ inch (3 mm). Line the bottom of a 9-inch (23 cm) pie tin. Bake in a 450°F (230°C) oven for 15 minutes. Cool.
2. Mix coffee and milk together in the top of a double boiler. Place over boiling water and scald mixture.
3. Beat egg yolks with sugar, salt, nutmeg and cinnamon. Add a little of the hot milk mixture, beating constantly. Return to double boiler and cook over simmering water until thick, stirring constantly.
4. Soak the gelatin in cold water for five minutes. Stir gelatin into coffee mixture until it dissolves. Add vanilla. Remove from heat and chill until partially set. Beat until fluffy.
5. Fold in egg whites. Pour into baked pie shell and chill until firm.
6. Before serving spread whipped cream over the top and sprinkle on grated chocolate.

Serves 6-8.

Rich Chocolate Pudding with Vanilla Sauce

1 cup sugar
2 tablespoons (40 g) butter or margarine
2 eggs
2 oz unsweetened chocolate
1 cup (250 ml) milk
1 cup flour
2 teaspoons baking powder

Sauce:
2 eggs, separated
1 cup confectioners' sugar
1 cup (250 ml) cream, whipped
1 teaspoon vanilla

1. For the pudding, beat together the sugar, butter or margarine and the beaten eggs. Add flour, baking powder, milk and melted chocolate. Mix well.
2. Pour pudding mixture in a baking dish and place in a pan of hot water. Cook in a 300°F (150°C) oven for 45 minutes.
3. To make sauce, beat the egg yolks until they are a pale yellow. Gradually add the sugar, whipped cream, vanilla and stiffly beaten egg whites.
4. Serve the pudding warm with the Vanilla Sauce over it.

Serves 6.

Chocolate Custard

2 oz unsweetened chocolate
1 cup (250 ml) milk
½ cup sugar
1½ tablespoons flour
¼ teaspoon salt
1 egg yolk, slightly beaten
1 teaspoon vanilla
½ cup (125 ml) cream, whipped

1. Melt chocolate in the top of a double boiler. Stir in milk and heat.
2. Add sugar, flour and salt and cook, stirring constantly, until thick. Stir in egg yolk and cook for two minutes.
3. Remove from heat. Add vanilla. Cool.
4. When cool, fold in whipped cream. Chill.

Serves 4.

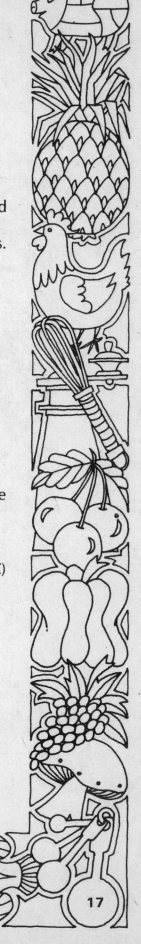

Oranges with Cream

4 large oranges
½ cup (125 ml) orange juice
sugar
1¼ cups (300 ml) cream, whipped

1. Grate the rind of one orange and mix into the orange juice.
2. Peel the oranges removing all the pith. Slice the oranges crosswise.
3. Place oranges in a shallow serving dish. Sprinkle with orange juice and sugar to taste.
4. Add a little sugar to the whipped cream and spoon over orange slices. Chill.

Serves 4.

Raisin Pudding

2 cups flour
pinch of salt
1 teaspoon baking powder
⅔ cup (166 g) butter
   or margarine
¼ lb (125 g) raisins

3 tablespoons sugar
1 teaspoon vanilla
2 eggs, well beaten
¾ cup (186 ml) milk
cream

1. Sift the flour with salt and baking powder. Rub in the butter or margarine until the mixture looks like fine bread crumbs.
2. Add the raisins, sugar and vanilla.
3. Add the eggs and gradually mix in the milk. Beat well.
4. Pour the mixture into a well-buttered cake tin. Bake in a 375°F (190°C) oven for ½ hour.
5. Serve warm with cream.

Serves 4-6.

Graham Cracker Torte

½ cup (125 g) butter
  or margarine
1 cup sugar
3 eggs, separated
1 teaspoon vanilla
grated rind of one orange
½ cup flour
2 teaspoons baking powder
½ lb (250 g) graham crackers,
  crushed
1 cup (250 ml) milk

Custard:
½ cup sugar
1 tablespoon cornstarch

⅛ teaspoon salt
2 egg yolks
1 cup (250 ml) milk, scalded
½ teaspoon vanilla

Icing:
2 cups confectioners' sugar
4 tablespoons (80 g) butter
  or margarine
4 tablespoons water
1 teaspoon vanilla
3 tablespoons cocoa

1. Cream together the butter or margarine and sugar. Add well-beaten egg yolks, vanilla and orange rind.
2. Add sifted dry ingredients and cracker crumbs alternately with the milk.
3. Beat egg whites until stiff and fold into mixture. Bake in two 8-inch (20 cm) sandwich tins in a 375°F (190°C) oven for 20 minutes. Cool.
4. To make custard filling, mix together the sugar, cornstarch and salt. Add slightly beaten egg yolks. Add the milk and mix well. Cook in the top of a double boiler over simmering water, stirring constantly, until smooth and thick. Cool. Add vanilla.
5. For icing, cream sugar and butter. Add water, vanilla and cocoa and mix well.
6. Spread custard between the two torte layers. Frost with icing.

Serves 6-8.

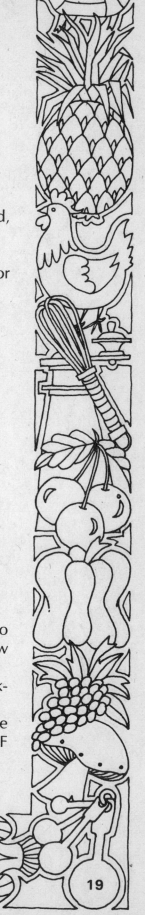

Carrot Pudding

½ cup (125 g) butter
  or margarine
½ cup brown sugar
1 egg, slightly beaten
1 cup grated raw corrots
2 teaspoons grated
  lemon rind
½ cup raisins

1 cup currants
1¼ cups flour
1 teaspoon baking powder
½ teaspoon salt
½ teaspoon nutmeg
½ teaspoon cinnamon
½ teaspoon baking
  soda

1. Mix together the butter or margarine, sugar, egg, carrot, lemon rind, raisins and currants.
2. Sift together the dry ingredients and mix with the carrot mixture.
3. Pour into a buttered casserole dish and bake in a 350°F (180°C) oven for about 1¼ hours or until firm.

Serves 6-8.

Lemon Bread Pudding

8 slices bread,
  crust removed
3 tablespoons lemon juice
grated rind of one lemon
¼ cup (62.5 g) butter
  or margarine
1 cup sugar
3 eggs, slightly beaten

Custard:
2 eggs, slightly beaten
1 cup (250 ml) milk
3 tablespoons sugar
⅛ teaspoon salt
grated rind of one lemon

1. Mix lemon juice, grated rind and butter in a saucepan. Cook for two minutes. Add sugar and eggs and cook, stirring constantly, over a low heat until thick. Cool.
2. Spread bread slices with the lemon mixture and place in a buttered baking dish.
3. Mix together the 2 eggs, milk, sugar, salt and lemon rind. Pour over the bread and allow to soak for 15 minutes. Cover and bake in a 350°F (180°C) oven for about one hour.

Serves 6.

Pavlova

4 egg whites	**Topping:**
1 cup sugar	1¼ cups (300 ml) cream,
½ teaspoon cornstarch	whipped
½ teaspoon vinegar	3 teaspoons confectioners' sugar
1 teaspoon vanilla	½ teaspoon vanilla
	strawberries

1. Beat the egg whites until stiff. Add the sugar a little at a time, beating well after each addition. Mix the cornstarch with the last amount of sugar. Fold in the vinegar and vanilla.
2. Put waxed paper on a greased baking tray. Sprinkle paper with cornstarch. Spread the meringue on the paper in the shape of a circle about 8 inches (20 cm) in diameter. Bake in a 250°F (120°C) for about 1½-2 hours or until the meringue is crisp. Turn oven off, open the door and allow the meringue to cool in the oven. Peel off paper.
3. Mix the confectioners' sugar and vanilla with the whipped cream. Spread on top of meringue.
4. Slice strawberries (or fruit of your choice) and place on top of whipped cream.

Serves 8-10.

Peaches Riviera

6 ripe peaches, peeled
½ pint strawberries
1 tablespoon lemon juice
1 tablespoon brandy
2 tablespoons sugar

1. Sieve the strawberries or purée in an electric blender.
2. Mix the strawberry purée with the lemon juice, brandy and sugar.
3. Pour over the peaches and chill well.

Serves 6.

Baked Lemon Pudding

½ cup sugar
1 cup flour
½ teaspoon baking powder
pinch of salt
2 eggs, separated
1 tablespoon grated
   lemon rind

3 tablespoons lemon juice
1½ tablespoons (30 g) butter
   or margarine, melted
1¼ cups (300 ml) milk

1. Sift together ¼ cup sugar, flour, baking powder and salt.
2. Beat the egg yolks until light. Add grated lemon rind, lemon juice, melted butter and milk. Beat well. Stir in the sifted dry ingredients and beat until smooth.
3. Beat the egg whites until stiff. Beat in the remaining ¼ cup sugar. Fold into the lemon mixture.
4. Pour into a well-buttered ovenproof dish in a pan of boiling water. Cook in a 350°F (180°C) oven for about 45 minutes.

Serves 6.

Milk Coffee Jelly

¼ cup sugar
½ cup (125 ml) strong coffee
1½ cups (375 ml) milk
1½ tablespoons gelatin
¼ cup cold water
½ teaspoon vanilla
whipped cream

1. Mix the sugar with the coffee and milk.
2. Soak the gelatin in the cold water for five minutes. Dissolve over hot water.
3. Mix the gelatin with the coffee mixture. Stir in the vanilla, pour into a mold and chill until firm.
4. Unmold and serve with whipped cream.

Serves 4.

Strawberry Cream Pie

Pastry:
1 cup flour
pinch of salt
¼ cup (62.5 g) butter
    or margarine
cold water

Filling:
1 cup sugar
6 tablespoons cornstarch
½ teaspoon salt
2½ cups (625 ml) milk,
    scalded
2 eggs slightly beaten
3 tablespoons (60 g) butter
    or margarine
1 teaspoon vanilla
1 pint strawberries
1 cup (250 ml) cream, whipped

1. Sift flour and salt into a mixing bowl. **Rub in** butter or margarine with your fingertips. Mix until mixture is the **consistency** of fine bread crumbs. Add enough cold water to form a stiff **dough. Roll** out to a thickness of ⅛ inch (3 mm) and line the bottom of a 9-inch (23 cm) pie tin. Bake in a 450°F (230°C) oven for 15 minutes.
2. For filling, mix sugar, cornstarch and **salt in the** top of a double boiler. Gradually add the milk and cook over **simmering** water, stirring constantly, until mixture is thick.
3. Add a little of the mixture to the beaten **eggs.** Pour back into double boiler and cook, stirring constantly, until thick.
4. Remove from heat and add butter and vanilla. Chill.
5. When cool, pour into baked pie shell. **Cover** with strawberries and chill well.
6. Just before serving spread whipped cream **over** the top.

Serves 8.

Lemon Chiffon Pie

Pastry:
1 cup plain flour
pinch of salt
¼ cup (62.5 g) butter
   or margarine
cold water

Filling:
4 egg yolks, beaten
½ cup sugar
½ cup lemon juice
½ teaspoon salt
1 tablespoon gelatin
¼ cup (62.5 ml) cold water
2 teaspoons grated
   lemon rind
½ cup sugar
4 egg whites, stiffly beaten
½ cup (125 ml) cream,
   whipped

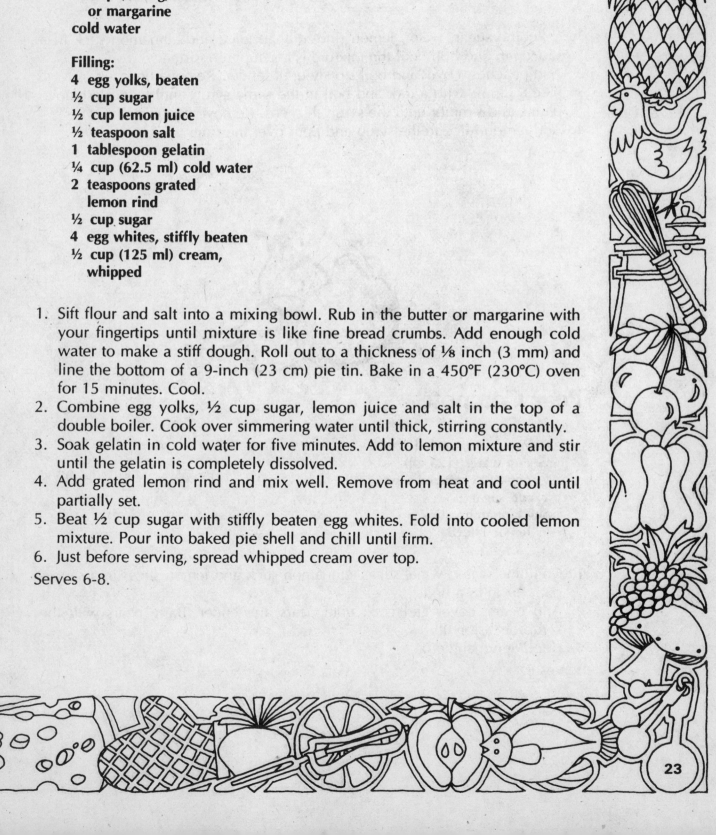

1. Sift flour and salt into a mixing bowl. Rub in the butter or margarine with your fingertips until mixture is like fine bread crumbs. Add enough cold water to make a stiff dough. Roll out to a thickness of ⅛ inch (3 mm) and line the bottom of a 9-inch (23 cm) pie tin. Bake in a 450°F (230°C) oven for 15 minutes. Cool.
2. Combine egg yolks, ½ cup sugar, lemon juice and salt in the top of a double boiler. Cook over simmering water until thick, stirring constantly.
3. Soak gelatin in cold water for five minutes. Add to lemon mixture and stir until the gelatin is completely dissolved.
4. Add grated lemon rind and mix well. Remove from heat and cool until partially set.
5. Beat ½ cup sugar with stiffly beaten egg whites. Fold into cooled lemon mixture. Pour into baked pie shell and chill until firm.
6. Just before serving, spread whipped cream over top.

Serves 6-8.

Plum and Peach Compote

1 cup sugar	one stick cinnamon
1 cup (250 ml) water	3 peaches, peeled
rind of ½ lemon	6 plums
juice of one orange	juice of one lemon

1. Combine sugar, water, lemon rind, orange juice and cinnamon stick in a saucepan and boil until the mixture is a syrupy consistency.
2. Add peaches, cover and boil slowly until tender. Remove peaches.
3. Pierce plums with a fork and boil in the same syrup until tender. Remove plums and simmer until the syrup thickens. Remove lemon rind.
4. Add lemon juice to the syrup and pour over the fruit.

Serves 4.

Pear Compote

6 firm pears, peeled
½ cup water (125 ml)
½ cup (125 ml) red wine
1 cup sugar
one cinnamon stick
½ lemon sliced

1. Combine water, wine, sugar, cinnamon stick and lemon slices in a saucepan. Bring to a boil.
2. Add pears, cover and cook until pears are tender. Baste pears with the syrup occasionally.
3. Cool. Serve chilled.

Serves 6.

Pumpkin Pudding

4 cups mashed cooked pumpkin	1½ teaspoons salt
2 cups brown sugar	2 tablespoons (40 g) butter or margarine, melted
1 cup white sugar	6 eggs, well beaten
light corn syrup	4 cups (1 liter) cream
1 tablespoon cinnamon	2 tablespoons brandy
2 teaspoons ginger	
1 teaspoon nutmeg	

1. Blend the pumpkin with one cup of the brown sugar, the white sugar, light corn syrup, cinnamon, ginger, nutmeg and salt. Then add the butter or margarine, eggs and cream. Stir in the brandy.
2. Butter a large casserole dish. Sprinkle remaining one cup of brown sugar on the bottom and pour in the pumpkin mixture.
3. Place casserole in a pan of boiling water and bake in a 350°F (180°C) oven for about 45 minutes or until set. Cool and chill until ready to serve. (May also be served warm with cream.)

Serves 8.

Banana Ice Cream

1 cup mashed bananas
1½ tablespoons lemon juice
pinch of salt
grated rind of ½ orange
2½ cups (625 ml) cream, whipped
confectioners' sugar to taste

1. Fold the bananas, lemon juice, salt and orange rind into the whipped cream.
2. Sweeten to taste with confectioners' sugar.
3. Pour into freezer tray and freeze until firm.

Serves 4.

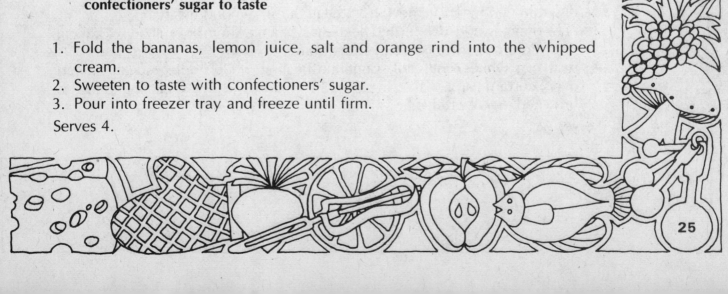

Apple Fritters with Melba Sauce

1 cup flour
¼ teaspoon salt
⅔ cup (166 ml) milk
2 eggs, separated
1 tablespoon (20 g) melted butter
    or margarine
sliced apple rings
confectioners' sugar

Sauce:
1 cup canned raspberries
    (or other berry)
½ cup (125 ml) currant jam
¼ cup sugar
2 teaspoons cornstarch
1 tablespoon cold water
2 teaspoons lemon juice

1. Sift flour and salt. Gradually add the milk with the beaten egg yolks and melted butter or margarine. Fold in the stiffly beaten egg whites.
2. Dip the apple rounds in the batter and fry in deep hot fat until brown. Drain.
3. To make the sauce, put berries, jam and sugar in a saucepan and bring to a boil. Blend cornstarch with water and lemon juice. Cook, stirring constantly, until clear. Strain through a sieve.

Serves 6.

Orange Custard

½ cup sugar
3 tablespoons cornstarch
pinch of salt
2½ cups (625 ml) milk,
    scalded

2 eggs, separated
2 tablespoons cream
½ teaspoon almond extract
4 oranges
⅓ cup sugar

1. In the top of a double boiler, mix the sugar, cornstarch and salt. Add milk, mix well and place over simmering water. Cook, stirring constantly, until thick.
2. Blend egg yolks with the cream and add to thickened mixture. Cook for one minute longer. Remove from heat. Stir in almond extract.
3. Peel oranges and divide into sections. Arrange them in a shallow baking dish. Pour custard mixture over the orange sections.
4. Beat egg whites until stiff. Continue beating while adding sugar. Spread over custard and bake in a 425°F (220°C) oven until meringue is browned. Serve chilled.

Serves 6.

Yoghurt Cheese Cake

Crust:
¾ lb (375 g) sweet plain
   cookies, crushed
½ cup (125 g) butter
   or margarine, melted
1 teaspoon cinnamon

Filling:
2 tablespoons gelatin
½ cup cold water
1 lb (500 g) cottage cheese

1 cup (250 g) yoghurt
4 eggs, separated
¾ cup sugar
pinch of salt
grated rind of one lemon
1 tablespoon lemon juice
1 cup sugar
1 cup (250 ml) cream,
   whipped

1. To make the crust, mix together the crushed cookies, melted butter or margarine and cinnamon. Firmly press the mixture on the bottom and sides of a 9-inch (23 cm) spring form pan. Chill.
2. Soften the gelatin in the cold water for five minutes.
3. Sieve the cottage cheese through a fine strainer or purée in an electric blender. Mix with the yoghurt.
4. In the top of a double boiler beat egg yolks with the sugar, salt and lemon rind until thick. Place over very hot water and cook for five minutes stirring constantly.
5. Add softened gelatin and stir until dissolved. Remove from heat and cool slightly.
6. Stir in lemon juice and yoghurt and cottage cheese mixture.
7. Beat egg whites until stiff. Gradually beat in the one cup of sugar. Fold into cheese mixture. Then fold in whipped cream.
8. Pour into crumb crust, cool and chill for several hours or overnight.

Serves 8.

Cherry Sponge Pie

Pastry:
2 cups plain flour
pinch of salt
½ cup (125 g) butter
   or margarine
cold water

Filling:
1 cup sugar
2 tablespoons cornstarch
½ teaspoon cinnamon

2 tablespoons lemon juice
2 cans sour cherries,
   pitted

Sponge batter:
2 tablespoons sugar
2 eggs, separated
2 tablespoons flour
pinch of salt
2 tablespoons water
½ teaspoon vanilla

1. For the pastry, sift together the flour and salt into a mixing bowl. Rub in the butter with your fingertips until mixture is like fine bread crumbs. Add enough cold water to make a stiff dough. Roll out to a thickness of ⅛ inch (3 mm) and line the bottom of two 23 cm (9-inch) pie tins. Bake in a 450°F (230°C) oven for fifteen minutes.
2. To make the filling, blend the sugar, cornstarch, cinnamon and lemon juice with liquid from the cherries in a saucepan. Cook until thick. Add cherries and boil for one minute. Pour into hot pastry shells.
3. For the sponge batter, beat the sugar and egg yolks together until light yellow colored. Sift the flour and salt and mix alternately with the stiffly beaten egg whites and water. Add vanilla.
4. Pour the batter over the cherry mixture in the pie shells and bake in a 375°F (190°C) oven for about fifteen minutes.

Serves 8.

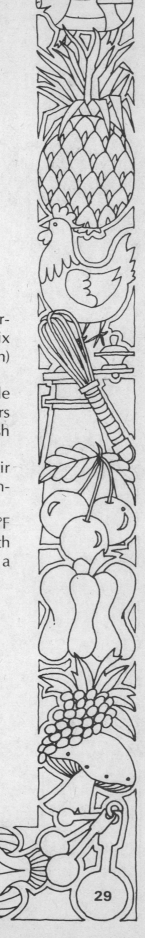

Apple Dumplings

6 apples
6 tablespoons sugar
cinnamon
1 stick of cinnamon
1 lemon rind

Pastry:
2 cups flour
4 teaspoons baking powder
½ teaspoon salt
⅓ cup (83 g) butter
  or margarine
¾ cup (186 ml) milk

Syrup:
2 cups white sugar
½ cup brown sugar
2 tablespoons cornstarch
½ teaspoon salt
2 cups (500 ml) boiling water
½ cup (125 g) butter
  or margarine

1. Sift flour, baking powder and salt into a mixing bowl. Add butter or margarine and mix in with a pastry blender or a fork. Add the milk and mix well. Roll the pastry ¼ inch (5 mm) thick and cut into six 6-inch (15 cm) squares.
2. Place a peeled and cored apple in the center of each square and sprinkle with one tablespoon of sugar and a little cinnamon. Bring up the corners of the pastry and pinch together firmly. Put in a well-buttered baking dish with the cinnamon stick and lemon rind.
3. In a saucepan mix together thoroughly the sugars, cornstarch and salt. Stir in the boiling water. Add butter or margarine and simmer, stirring constantly, until thick and smooth.
4. Pour the syrup over the apple dumplings, cover and bake in a 425°F (220°C) oven for about ½ hour. Remove cover, baste the dumplings with the syrup and continue to bake, uncovered, until the dumplings are a golden brown. Serve hot.

Serves 6.

Coconut Oranges

8 large oranges, peeled
1½ cups (375 ml) orange juice
½ cup (125 ml) pineapple juice
½ cup (125 ml) lemon juice
1 cup sugar
shredded coconut

1. Mix together orange, pineapple and lemon juices. Stir in sugar and bring to a boil. Boil for ten minutes.
2. Put oranges into syrup and boil for 1-2 minutes, turning constantly. Drain but reserve syrup.
3. Chill oranges. Before serving roll oranges in coconut and spoon some syrup over the top.

Serves 8.

Glazed Apple Squares

½ cup (125 g) butter
  or margarine
2 tablespoons sugar
2 eggs, well beaten
1 cup (250 ml) milk
2 cups flour
¼ teaspoon salt
4 teaspoons baking powder
4 apples, peeled,
  cored and sliced

Topping:
½ cup (125 g) butter
  or margarine
1 cup confectioners' sugar
½ teaspoon vanilla

1. Cream ½ cup butter or margarine with the two tablespoons sugar. Add eggs and sifted dry ingredients alternately with the milk. Pour into a shallow greased and floured baking tin. Cover with the sliced apples and bake in a 350°F (180°C) oven for about 45 minutes.
2. For topping, mix together the ½ cup butter or margarine with the confectioners' sugar and vanilla. Spread over the hot cake. Cool and cut into squares.

Serves 6-8.

Pineapple Cottage Cheese Cake

Crust:
2 cups finely crushed
   corn flakes
½ cup (125 g) butter
   or margarine, melted
3 tablespoons sugar
1 tablespoon cinnamon

Filling:
2 tablespoons gelatin
½ cup cold water
3 eggs, separated

½ cup sugar
⅛ teaspoon salt
1 cup (250 ml) milk
1 lb (500 g) cottage cheese
juice of ½ lemon
grated rind of ½ lemon
1 teaspoon vanilla
¾ cup crushed
   pineapple
½ cup (125 ml) cream,
   whipped

1. To make the crust, mix together the corn flake crumbs, melted butter or margarine, sugar and cinnamon. Press firmly on the bottom and sides of a spring form pan. Reserve a little of the crust to sprinkle on top of cake.
2. Soak the gelatin in the cold water for five minutes.
3. In the top of a double boiler, beat the egg yolks with the sugar and salt. Stir in milk and place over simmering water. Cook, stirring constantly, until mixture is creamy.
4. Add the gelatin and stir until gelatin is completely dissolved.
5. Mix in the cottage cheese, lemon juice and rind, vanilla and pineapple. Fold in stiffly beaten egg whites and whipped cream. Pour into crust and chill until firm.

Serves 8.

Baked Peaches

6 large ripe peaches	½ cup (125 ml) water
2 tablespoons (40 g) butter or margarine	1 cup sugar
	juice of one lemon
½ teaspoon cinnamon	grated rind of one lemon
¼ teaspoon nutmeg	¼ cup (62.5 ml) brandy

1. Peel peaches and put into a glass baking dish.
2. Add butter or margarine, cinnamon, nutmeg, water, sugar, lemon juice, grated rind and brandy.
3. Bake in a 400°F (200°C) oven for about 30 minutes. Serve hot or cold.

Serves 6.

Lemon Fluff Refrigerator Cake

Crust:	½ cup cold water
¾ lb graham crackers, crushed	6 eggs, separated
⅓ cup (83 g) butter or margarine, melted	2 cups sugar
	3 lemons, juice and grated rind
1 teaspoon cinnamon	¼ teaspoon salt
1 tablespoon sugar	

Filling:
2 tablespoons gelatin

1. Mix together the cracker crumbs, butter, cinnamon and sugar. Firmly press mixture on bottom and sides of a large spring form pan.
2. Soak the gelatin in the water for five minutes.
3. In the top of a double boiler, beat the egg yolks and 1 cup of sugar until light. Add the lemon juice, grated rind and gelatin mixture. Cook over simmering water until thick, stirring constantly. Cool.
4. Add salt to egg whites and beat until stiff. Fold in remaining cup of sugar and the cooled lemon mixture. Pour into spring form pan and chill until firm.

Serves 8.

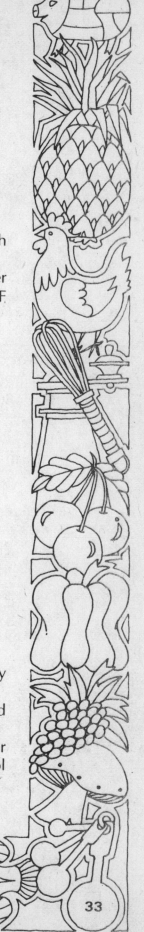

Raspberry Pudding

4 cups raspberries
2 tablespoons lemon juice
¼ teaspoon cinnamon
1 cup flour
1 cup sugar
½ cup (125 g) butter
   or margarine
whipped cream

1. Wash and drain the berries. Put them in a baking dish and sprinkle with the lemon juice and cinnamon.
2. Sift flour and sugar and mix in the butter or margarine with a pastry mixer or a knife. Spread over the raspberries. Bake for 45-50 minutes in a 400°F (200°C) oven.
3. Serve warm with whipped cream.

Serves 6.

Nutty Cheese Cake

Crust:
½ lb (250 g) graham crackers
   crushed
½ cup (125 g) butter
   or margarine, melted
1 teaspoon cinnamon
1 tablespoon sugar

Filling:
⅔ cup sugar

4 eggs
¼ teaspoon salt
1 cup (250 ml) cream, whipped
1½ lb (750 g) cottage cheese
2 tablespoons lemon juice
grated rind of one lemon
4 tablespoons flour
½ cup (60 g) chopped nuts

1. Mix cracker crumbs, melted butter, cinnamon and sugar together. Firmly press on the bottom and sides of a 9-inch (23 cm) spring form pan.
2. Beat eggs and sugar until light and fluffy. Add salt, lemon juice, grated rind, cream, cheese, flour and nuts. Blend thoroughly.
3. Pour mixture into spring form pan and cook in a 350°F (180°C) oven for about one hour or until cake is firm. Turn off heat and allow cake to cool in the oven.

Serves 8.

Butterscotch Crumb Pie

Pastry:
1 cup plain flour
pinch salt
¼ cup (62.5 g) butter
  or margarine
cold water

Filling:
2 egg yolks
¾ cup brown sugar, packed
1 cup (250 ml) milk, scalded
pinch of salt

2 tablespoons (40 g) butter
  or margarine
1 tablespoon gelatin
¼ cup (62.5 g) cold water
1 teaspoon vanilla
2 egg whites, stiffly
  beaten
2 tablespoons sugar
¼ lb (125 g) peanut brittle,
  crushed
½ cup (125 ml) cream, whipped

1. Sift flour and salt into a mixing bowl. Rub in the butter or margarine with your fingertips until the mixture is like fine bread crumbs. Add enough water to make a stiff dough. Roll out to a thickness of ⅛ inch (3 mm). Bake in a 450°F (230°C) oven for 15 minutes. Cool.
2. Beat egg yolks and brown sugar until thick in the top of a double boiler.
3. Slowly add the hot milk, stirring constantly. Place over simmering water and cook, stirring constantly, until thick. Add salt and butter and continue cooking.
4. Soak the gelatin in cold water for five minutes. Stir into the custard mixture until gelatin dissolves.
5. Remove from heat and add the vanilla. Cool until partially set.
6. Beat the 2 tablespoons of sugar into the stiffly beaten egg whites. Fold into gelatin mixture. Fold in the peanut brittle and whipped cream.
7. Pour into baked pie shell and chill until firm.

Serves 6-8.

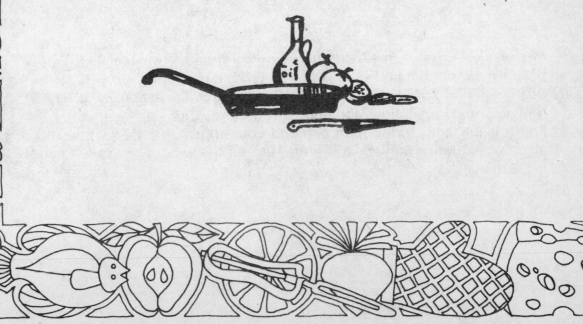

Apple Cheese Strudel

Pastry:
1 cup (250 g) sweet
   butter
½ lb (250 g) cottage cheese
2 cups flour

Filling:
2 cups pie apples
½ cup sugar

1 teaspoon cinnamon
1 teaspoon nutmeg
½ cup (87 g) chopped peel
½ teaspoon salt
blanched almonds
1 egg, beaten

1. Mix the butter, cottage cheese and flour in a mixing bowl. Chill for ½ hour. Roll out to a large oblong (not too thin).
2. Mix apples with the sugar, cinnamon, nutmeg, peel and salt. Spread over pastry.
3. Glaze all edges of pastry with beaten egg. Tuck in ends of pastry and fold over. Brush top of roll with egg and sprinkle with chopped almonds.
4. Bake in a 375°F (190°C) oven for 30-45 minutes or until golden brown.

Serves 6-8.

Coffee Freeze

3 tablespoons cornstarch
1 cup sugar
¼ teaspoon salt
⅓ cup (83 ml) cream
3 egg yolks, well beaten
1½ cups strong coffee
2½ cups (625 ml) cream, whipped

1. In the top of a double boiler, combine the cornstarch, sugar and salt. Slowly stir in ⅓ cup cream. Mix well.
2. Add the egg yolks and then the coffee. Cook over simmering water until thick, stirring constantly. Cool.
3. Fold in the whipped cream and pour into a tray. Freeze until solid.

Serves 6.

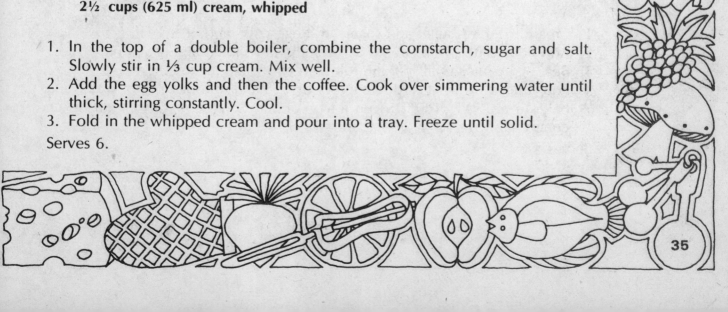

Apple Swirls

Pastry:
1½ cups plain flour
¼ cup (62.5 g) butter
  or margarine
2 teaspoons baking powder
2 tablespoons sugar
⅓ cup (83 ml) milk
½ teaspoon salt

Filling:
2 cups finely
  chopped apples

½ cup raisins
1 tablespoon grated
  lemon rind

Syrup:
1 cup (250 ml) water
½ cup sugar
1 tablespoon maple syrup
  or corn syrup

1. Combine flour, butter or margarine, baking powder, sugar, milk and salt. Mix well. Roll into a rectangular shape about ⅓ inch (7 mm) thick.
2. Spread apples over the pastry. Sprinkle with raisins and lemon rind. Dot with butter or margarine and roll up lengthwise. Cut into 1½ inch (4 cm) rounds.
3. Mix together the water, sugar and syrup in a saucepan and bring to a boil. Pour into a baking dish.
4. Place rounds in the dish with the syrup and bake in a 375°F (190°C) oven until golden brown.

Serves 6-8.

Chocolate Fluff

1 tablespoon (20 g)
  butter or margarine
½ cup sugar
2 eggs, separated

1 tablespoon flour
1 tablespoon cocoa
1 cup (250 ml) milk
1 teaspoon vanilla

1. Cream together butter and sugar. Add egg yolks and beat well.
2. Add flour, sifted with cocoa. Stir in milk and vanilla and beat well.
3. Beat egg whites until stiff and fold into chocolate mixture.
4. Pour into a well-buttered ovenproof dish. Stand in a pan of hot water and bake in a 350°F (180°C) oven for one hour. Serve hot with cream or ice cream.

Serves 4-6.

Banana Puffs

8 bananas

Pastry:
2 cups flour
pinch of salt
½ cup (125 g) butter
　or margarine
cold water

Sauce:
½ cup sugar

1 tablespoon flour
⅛ teaspoon salt
1 cup (250 ml) boiling water
juice of one lemon
grated rind of ½ lemon
1½ tablespoons (30 g)
　butter or margarine
3 tablespoons raisins

1. Sift flour and salt into a mixing bowl. Rub in butter or margarine with your fingertips until mixture is like fine bread crumbs. Add enough water to make a firm dough. Chill. Roll out to a thickness of ⅛ inch (3 mm).
2. Peel bananas and roll in sugar and cinnamon. Wrap in pastry pinching the edges together. Bake in a 450°F (230°C) oven for 15 minutes.
3. In the top of a double boiler mix together the sugar, flour, salt and water. Cook over simmering water for ten minutes. Add lemon juice, lemon rind, butter and raisins and mix well.
4. Pour hot sauce over the pastry-wrapped bananas.

Serves 8.

Fruit Flan

Pastry:
½ cup (125 g) butter
  or margarine
½ cup sugar
1 egg
2 cups flour
1½ teaspoons baking powder
pinch of salt

Filling:
1 packet blackberry gelatin
1 large can fruit
  (of your choice)
⅔ cup (166 ml) cream

1. Cream together butter or margarine and sugar. Add egg and beat well. Sift flour, baking powder and salt and add to mixture. (Pastry should be dry.) Roll out and line a 10-inch (25 cm) square tin and bake in a 350°F (180°C) oven until a pale golden color. Remove from tin and cool.
2. Make gelatin by heating the syrup from the drained fruit and make up to 2 cups with boiling water. Add gelatin and stir until dissolved. Cool.
3. When gelatin begins to thicken, add fruit and pour into baked and cooled pastry shell.
4. When ready to serve, whip cream and spread over the top of the flan.

Serves 6-8.

Apples Baked in Cream

6 large cooking apples
3 tablespoons (60 g) butter
  or margarine
1 cup sugar
½ cup (125 ml) cream
1 teaspoon cinnamon
½ teaspoon nutmeg

1. Peel and core the apples. Slice into ½ inch (1 cm) rounds.
2. Place apples in a well-buttered oven-proof dish. Dot with butter or margarine.
3. Combine sugar, cream, cinnamon and nutmeg and pour over the apples.
4. Bake in a 350°F (180°C) oven for 30 minutes.

Serves 6.

Chocolate Torte

2 oz (60 g) unsweetened
  chocolate
½ cup (125 g) butter
¾ cup sugar
2 eggs
¾ cup flour
¼ teaspoon baking powder
pinch of salt
½ teaspoon vanilla
½ cup (60 g) chopped
  walnuts

2 tablespoons instant coffee
3 tablespoons sugar
¼ teaspoon ground cloves
1 tablespoon sherry
1 cup (250 ml) hot water

Cream:
1 cup (250 ml) cream
½ teaspoon vanilla
1 egg white, stiffly beaten
2 tablespoons sugar

Filling:
2 tablespoons cornstarch

1. Melt the chocolate. Cool.
2. Cream together the butter and sugar. Add eggs.
3. Add flour, baking powder and a pinch of salt to the egg mixture. Mix thoroughly. Add the melted chocolate, vanilla and walnuts and mix well.
4. Butter four 8-inch (20 cm) cake tins and line with buttered waxed paper.
5. Spread the mixture evenly over the four tins. Cook in a 400°F (200°C) oven for 15 minutes. Cool.
6. Combine all ingredients for the filling, except the water, in a saucepan. Slowly add the water, stirring constantly. Cook over a low heat until thick. Cool.
7. For the cream, whip cream with the vanilla. Beat sugar into the stiffly beaten egg whites. Fold in whipped cream.
8. Assemble torte, alternating cake, filling and cream.

Serves 8.

Chocolate Chip Pudding

2 egg yolks
3 tablespoons sugar
⅔ cup (166 ml) milk
pinch of salt
1 tablespoon gelatin
¼ cup (62.5 ml) cold water

1 teaspoon vanilla
2 egg whites, stiffly beaten
3 tablespoons sugar
½ cup coarsely chipped cooking chocolate
1 cup (250 ml) cream, whipped

1. Beat egg yolks and sugar together. Add milk and salt and mix well. Cook in top of a double boiler over simmering water until thick, stirring constantly.
2. Soak gelatin in cold water for five minutes. Add to egg and milk mixture with the vanilla. Stir until gelatin dissolves. Chill until partially set.
3. Add sugar to stiffly beaten egg whites and beat well.
4. Fold egg whites and chocolate chips into gelatin mixture and pour into a serving dish. Chill until firm.

Serves 6.

Strawberry Whip

1 tablespoon gelatin
¼ cup (62.5 ml) cold water
½ cup (125 ml) hot water
½ cup sugar
3 tablespoons lemon juice
4 tablespoons orange juice
pinch of salt
1 pint strawberries
1 egg white, stiffly beaten

1. Soak gelatin in cold water for five minutes. Dissolve in hot water.
2. Add sugar, fruit juices and salt and chill until partially set. Beat until frothy.
3. Crush strawberries (reserve some for decoration) and add to gelatin mixture. Fold in egg white.
4. Chill in an oiled mold until firm. Unmold and garnish with whole strawberries.

Serves 4-6.

Chocolate Fluff Pudding

½ cup sugar
2 tablespoons flour
⅛ teaspoon salt
2 egg yolks, beaten
1 beaten egg
2 cup (500 ml) milk, scalded
1 teaspoon vanilla

½ cup confectioners' sugar
2 egg whites, stiffly beaten
1 oz (30 g) semi-sweet chocolate, melted
½ teaspoon vanilla
⅛ teaspoon salt

1. In the top of a double boiler combine sugar, flour, salt, egg yolks and the beaten egg. Gradually add milk, stirring constantly.
2. Place over simmering water and cook, stirring constantly, until thickened. Cool and add vanilla.
3. Pour into individual dishes and chill.
4. Beat sugar into egg whites until sugar is dissolved.
5. Slowly add melted chocolate, vanilla and salt. Chill.
6. When ready to serve top pudding with chocolate fluff.

Serves 6.

Vanilla Wafer Dessert

1 cup (250 ml) unsweetened pineapple juice
½ cup (125 ml) orange juice
2 tablespoons lemon juice
pinch of salt
24 marshmallows, quartered
1 cup (250 ml) cream, whipped
20 vanilla wafers

1. Combine fruit juices and salt. Heat to boiling.
2. Add marshmallows and stir until melted. Chill until slightly thickened. Fold in whipped cream.
3. Alternate layers of wafers and marshmallow mixture in a rectangular dish. (Use wafers for top and bottom layers.) Chill until firm. Cut into squares.

Serves 6.

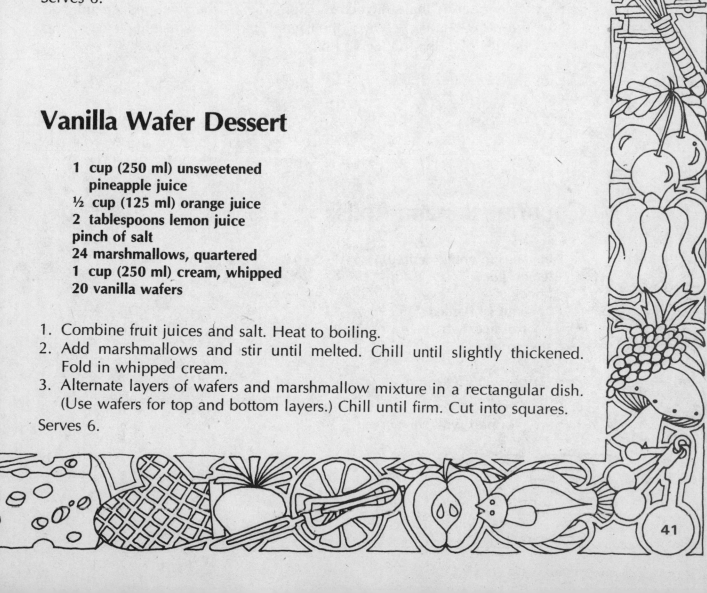

Strawberry Shortcake

2 cups flour
½ teaspoon salt
4 teaspoons baking powder
1 tablespoon sugar
⅓ cup (83 g) butter
1 egg, well beaten
½ cup (125 ml) milk
1 pint strawberries
whipped cream

1. Sift dry ingredients. Mix in butter until mixture is like coarse crumbs.
2. Combine egg and milk and stir into flour and butter mixture. Mix until just moistened.
3. Turn out onto a slightly floured surface. Divide dough in half. Pat out to fit an 8-inch (20 cm) cake tin. Brush with melted butter. Repeat with second half.
4. Bake in a 450°F (230°C) oven for about 15 minutes.
5. Stem and quarter the strawberries. Spread half the whipped cream and half the strawberries between the layers and the remaining cream and strawberries over the top. Serve hot.

Serves 6.

Coconut Banana Rolls

bananas (number desired)
lemon juice
honey
coconut (shredded
    or desiccated)
sour cream

1. Peel bananas. Dip in lemon juice and honey.
2. Cover with coconut.
3. Serve topped with sour cream.

Cherry Dessert Cake

3 eggs
1 cup sugar
1¾ cups flour
¼ teaspoon salt
2 teaspoons baking powder
2 tablespoons water
1 teaspoon vanilla
¼ teaspoon almond extract
1½ cups pitted fresh
    cherries
½ cup (60 g) chopped
    walnuts
1 cup (250 ml) cream, whipped

1. Beat eggs until light. Gradually add sugar and beat until lemon colored.
2. Add sifted dry ingredients and mix well.
3. Add water, vanilla and almond extract and mix thoroughly.
4. Pour mixture into two 9-inch (23 cm) cake tins lined with waxed paper.
5. Drop cherries and nuts over batter.
6. Bake in a 350°F (180°C) oven for 30 minutes.
7. Serve with whipped cream between layers and over top.

Serves 8.

Date Pudding

3 eggs, beaten
1 cup sugar
¼ cup flour
¼ teaspoon salt
1 teaspoon baking powder
1 cup (150 g) chopped dates
1 cup (120 g) coarsely
    chopped walnuts

1. Beat eggs and sugar until light.
2. Add sifted dry ingredients and mix well.
3. Stir in dates and nuts.
4. Pour into a greased 8-inch square pan and bake in a pan of hot water in a 350°F (180°C) oven for one hour. Serve warm.

Serves 6.

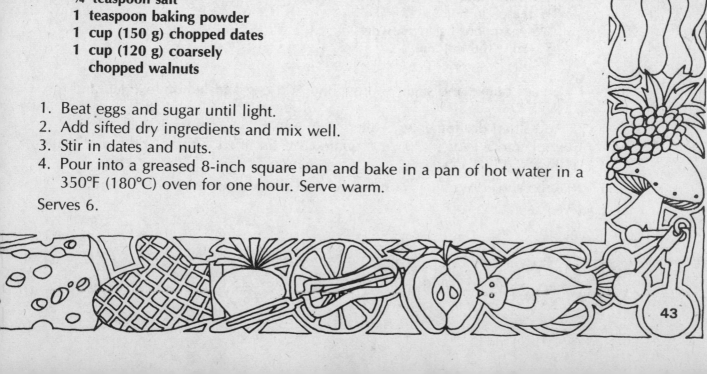

Brown Betty

2 cups dry bread crumbs
3 tablespoons (60 g) melted
   butter or margarine
4 medium apples, peeled,
   cored and sliced
1½ tablespoons lemon juice
1 teaspoon grated lemon rind
½ cup brown sugar
⅓ cup (83 ml) hot water

1. Mix together crumbs and butter and stir over low heat until lightly browned. Place ⅓ of mixture in a greased baking dish.
2. Arrange half the apple slice over the crumbs. Sprinkle with half the lemon juice, grated rind and sugar.
3. Add second layer or crumbs, remaining apples, lemon juice and rind and sugar. Cover with remaining crumbs. Pour water over it all.
4. Bake in a 375°F (190°C) oven for 30-40 minutes or until apples are tender.

Serves 6.

Cottage Pudding

¼ cup (62.5 g) butter
   or margarine
1 cup sugar
1 egg
½ teaspoon lemon extract
1¾ cups flour
½ teaspoon salt
2½ teaspoons baking powder
⅔ cup (166 ml) milk

1. Cream butter and sugar thoroughly. Add egg and lemon extract and mix well.
2. Add sifted dry ingredients alternately with milk. Beat well.
3. Pour into a 8-inch (20 cm) square cake tin lined with waxed paper. Bake in a 350°F (180°C) oven for 35-45 minutes.

(May be served with fresh or canned fruit.)

Serves 6.

Mocha Cream Pie

Pastry:
1 cup plain flour
pinch of salt
¼ cup (62.5 g) butter
   or margarine
cold water

Filling:
½ cup sugar
6 tablespoons flour
2 tablespoons instant
   coffee powder

1½ teaspoons cinnamon
1 teaspoon cloves
3 cups (750 ml) milk
3 egg yolks, beaten
3 tablespoons (60 g) butter
   or margarine
6 oz (185 g) semi-sweet chocolate
1 teaspoon vanilla
1¼ cups (300 ml) cream, whipped

1. Sift flour and salt into a mixing bowl. Rub in the butter or margarine with your fingertips until the mixture is the consistency of fine bread crumbs. Add enough cold water to form a stiff dough. Roll out to a thickness of ⅛ inch (3 mm) and line the bottom of a 9-inch (23 cm) pie tin. Bake in a 450°F (230°C) oven for 15 minutes.
2. Mix together the sugar, flour, coffee, cinnamon and cloves. Gradually add the cold milk, stirring until the mixture is smooth. Cook over low heat, stirring constantly, until thickened.
3. Blend in the beaten egg yolks, butter or margarine and the chocolate. Cook over low heat for five minutes. Remove from heat and stir in the vanilla. Cool. Pour into baked pie shell and chill until firm.
4. Before serving spread whipped cream over the top.

Serves 8.

Lemon Soufflé Bread Pudding

2 cups bread cubes
   (without crusts)
¾ cup sugar
juice and grated rind of
   one lemon
½ cup (125 g) butter
   or margarine
4 eggs separated
⅔ cup (166 ml) milk

1. Mix together bread cubes, sugar, juice and rind of lemon.
2. Melt butter or margarine and stir into bread cubes.
3. Beat egg yolks until thick and lemon-colored. Add milk and pour over bread cubes.
4. Beat egg whites until stiff and fold into bread mixture.
5. Pour into a buttered casserole dish and bake in a 350°F (180°C) oven for ½ hour. Serve warm.

Serves 6.

Banana Fluff Pudding

1 tablespoon gelatin
¼ cup (62.5 ml) cold water
5 medium bananas, mashed
1 cup (250 ml) orange juice
2 tablespoons lemon juice
1 tablespoon grated
   orange rind
pinch of salt
¾ cup confectioners' sugar
1 cup cream, whipped

1. Soak the gelatin in the cold water for five minutes. Dissolve over hot water.
2. Mix together the mashed bananas, lemon juice, orange juice, rind, salt and sugar.
3. Add gelatin and mix well. Chill until slightly thickened.
4. Fold in whipped cream and chill well.

Serves 6-8.

Frozen Vanilla Custard

     2 cups (500 ml) milk
     3 eggs, beaten
     ¾ cup sugar
     ⅛ teaspoon salt
     1 cup (250 ml) cream, whipped
     1 tablespoon vanilla

1. Heat milk in the top of double boiler over boiling water.
2. Mix together eggs, sugar and salt. Gradually stir in the hot milk, mixing constantly.
3. Return over double boiler and cook over simmering water, stirring constantly, until mixture thickens.
4. Remove from heat and cool.
5. When cooled, fold in whipped cream and vanilla. Pour into trays and freeze until firm.

Serves 6.

Frozen Lemon Mousse

     2 tablespoons cornstarch
     ¼ teaspoon salt
     1 cup sugar
     1 cup (250 ml) milk
     3 egg yolks, slightly beaten
     ½ cup lemon juice
     grated rind of one lemon
     2½ cups (625 ml) cream, whipped

1. Mix together cornstarch, salt and sugar in the top of a double boiler. Add milk, mix well and cook over boiling water for about 15 minutes, stirring occasionally.
2. Pour hot milk mixture slowly over egg yolks, stirring constantly. Mix well and return to double boiler. Cook over simmering water for one minute. Add lemon juice and rind and remove from heat. Chill.
3. Fold in whipped cream and pour into freezer trays. Freeze until firm.

Serves 8.

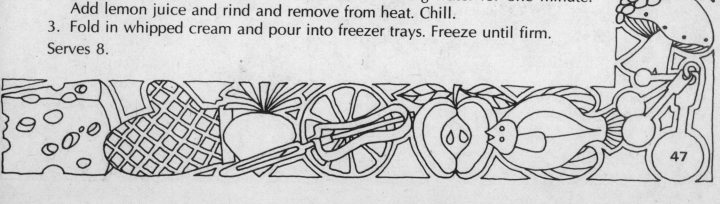

Cottage Cheese Pie

Pastry:
1 cup flour
pinch of salt
¼ cup (62.5 g) butter
   or margarine
cold water

Filling:
¾ lb (375 g) cottage cheese
1 tablespoon flour
¼ teaspoon salt
1 cup (250 ml) cream
½ cup sugar
grated rind of one lemon
juice of one lemon
3 eggs, separated
½ cup dried currants
confectioners' sugar

1. Sift flour and salt into a mixing bowl. Rub in butter or margarine with your fingertips until mixture looks like fine bread crumbs. Add enough cold water to form a stiff dough. Chill. Roll out to a thickness of ⅛ inch (3 mm) and line bottom of a 9-inch (23 cm) pie tin.
2. Sieve cottage cheese through a fine strainer. Blend in flour and salt. Stir in cream, sugar, lemon rind and lemon juice.
3. Beat egg whites until stiff.
4. Beat egg yolks well and mix with cheese mixture.
5. Stir currants into cheese mixture.
6. Fold in egg whites and pour into pastry shell.
7. Bake in a 450°F (230°C) oven for 10 minutes. Reduce heat to 350°F (180°C) and bake for about 45 minutes or until firm.
8. Cool and sprinkle with confectioners' sugar.

Serves 6-8.

Sour Cream Raisin Pie

Pastry:
2 cups flour
pinch salt
½ cup (125 g) butter
    or margarine
cold water

Filling:
2 eggs

1 cup sugar
1 cup (250 g) sour cream
1 cup raisins
¼ teaspoon nutmeg
⅛ salt
1½ tablespoons lemon juice

1. Sift flour and salt into a mixing bowl. Rub in butter or margarine with your fingertips until mixture looks like fine bread crumbs. Add enough cold water to form a stiff dough. Halve the dough. Roll out one half to a thickness of ⅛ inch (3 mm) and line the bottom of a 9-inch (23 cm) pie tin.
2. Beat eggs slightly. Add sugar and beat until light.
3. Add sour cream, raisins, nutmeg, salt and lemon juice and mix well. Pour into unbaked crust.
4. Roll out other half and cover pie. Make slits with a knife to allow steam to escape. Press edges together.
5. Bake in a 450°F (230°C) oven for 15 minutes. Reduce heat to 350°F (180°C) and bake for 30 minutes longer.

Serves 6-8.

Apple Mousse

4 large cooking apples,
    peeled, cored and cut up
grated rind of one lemon
4 tablespoons lemon juice

1 tablespoon gelatin
3 eggs
1¼ cups (300 ml) cream
3 tablespoons sugar

1. Cook the apples with the lemon rind and a little water. Drain and sieve through a fine strainer.
2. Soak the gelatin in the lemon juice for five minutes. Heat gently to dissolve the gelatin. When mixture begins to thicken add to the apple.
3. Beat the eggs over boiling water until thick and creamy. Cool.
4. Add cooled eggs to the apple mixture with the sugar.
5. Fold in the cream. Pour into a wet mold or cake tin and chill until firm.

Serves 6.

Rhubarb Pie

Pastry:
2 cups flour
pinch of salt
½ cup (125 g) butter
  or margarine
cold water

Filling:
3 tablespoons flour

1 cup sugar
pinch of salt
4 cups diced rhubarb
grated rind of one
  orange
¼ cup (62.5 ml) orange
  juice
2 tablespoons butter
  or margarine

1. Sift flour and salt into a mixing bowl. Rub in the butter or margarine with your fingertips until mixture is the consistency of dried bread crumbs. Add enough water to form a dough. Roll out half the dough and line the bottom of a 9-inch (23 cm) pie tin.
2. Mix flour, sugar, salt and rhubarb. Add grated orange rind and juice. Put into bottom crust, dot with butter.
3. Roll out other half of dough and cut into strips. Cover pie with strips, lattice fashion. Bake for 20 minutes in a 450°F (230°C) oven then reduce heat to 350°F (180°C) and cook for another 20 minutes.

Serves 6-8.

Russian Cream

1 cup (250 ml) heavy cream
¾ cup sugar
1½ teaspoons gelatin
2 tablespoons cold water

1 cup (250 g) sour cream
fresh strawberries
  (or other fruit)

1. Combine cream and sugar and heat in the top of a double boiler.
2. Soak the gelatin in the cold water for five minutes. Add to the cream and stir until dissolved. Remove from heat and cool.
3. Beat sour cream and fold into gelatin and cream mixture.
4. Pour into individual molds and chill until firm.
5. Unmold and serve with fresh strawberries.

Serves 4.

Lemon Meringue Pie

Pastry:
1 cup flour
pinch of salt
¼ cup (62.5 g) butter
   or margarine
cold water

Filling:
3 tablespoons cornstarch

½ cup (125 ml) water
juice of two lemons
grated rind of one lemon
½ cup sugar
2 eggs, separated
½ cup sugar

1. Sift the flour and salt into a mixing bowl. Rub in butter or margarine with your fingertips until mixture is the consistency of fine bread crumbs. Add enough cold water to form a stiff dough. Chill before rolling out. Roll out to a thickness of ⅛ inch (3 mm). Line a 7-inch (18 cm) flan case or a deep pie tin. Bake in a 450°F (230°C) oven for 15 minutes.
2. Mix the lemon juice and grated rind and bring to a boil, stirring until mixture thickens. Add sugar and mix well. Remove from heat. Cool slightly. Add the beaten egg yolks and pour into the baked pastry shell.
3. Beat the egg whites until stiff, beat in the sugar. Spread on top of lemon mixture and bake in center of the oven until the meringue is lightly browned.

Serves 6.

Orange Ambrosia

6 oranges
sugar
desiccated coconut
brandy

1. Peel the oranges and slice very thinly.
2. Layer the oranges, sugar and coconut in a serving dish. Pour over the brandy and chill for one hour.

Serves 6.

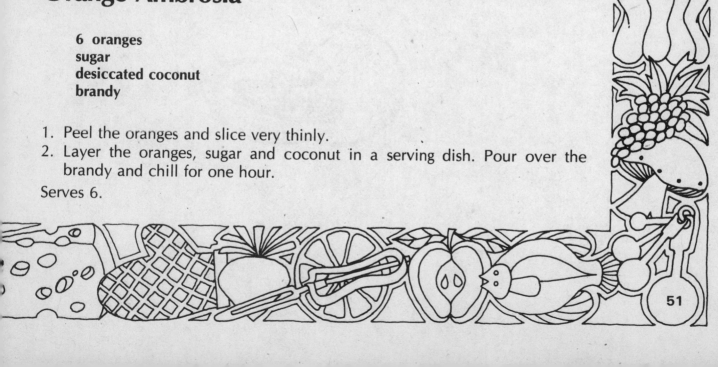

Butterscotch Cream Pie

Pastry:
1 cup flour
pinch of salt
¼ cup (62.5 g) butter
    or margarine
cold water

Filling:
½ cup sugar

⅓ cup hot water
2 cups (500 ml) milk
¼ cup (62.5 g) butter
    or margarine
6 tablespoons flour
¾ cup brown sugar, packed
½ teaspoon salt
2 eggs
1 cup (250 ml) cream, whipped

1. Sift the flour and salt into a mixing bowl. Rub in butter or margarine with your fingertips until mixture is the consistency of fine bread crumbs. Add enough water to form a stiff dough. Roll out to a thickness of ⅛ inch (3 mm), line a pie tin and bake in a 450°F (230°C) oven for 15 minutes.
2. Put sugar in a small saucepan and cook, without stirring, until sugar melts and becomes golden brown. Remove from heat and slowly add water. Cook, without stirring, until sugar dissolves. Add milk and heat almost to the boiling point. Remove from heat.
3. Melt the butter or margarine in the top of a double boiler. Remove from heat and add mixture of flour, brown sugar and salt. Beat eggs and add to the double boiler.
4. Slowly add the caramel and milk mixture and cook over boiling water until thickened, stirring constantly. Cover and cook for ten more minutes.
5. Cool. Pour into baked pie shell and chill for several hours. Spread whipped cream over the top.

Serves 6-8.

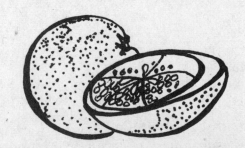

Lemon-Apple Cheese Cake

Crust:
1 cup graham cracker
  crumbs
2 tablespoons brown
  sugar
¼ cup (62.5 g) butter
  or margarine, melted
½ cup (60 g) chopped walnuts

Filling:
1 ⅔ cups (416 ml)
  evaporated milk

1 packet lemon gelatin
1 tablespoon unflavored
  gelatin
¾ cup (186 ml) boiling water
½ lb (250 g) cream cheese
¾ cup sugar
2 cups puréed apples
1 teaspoon vanilla

1. Mix crumbs, brown sugar, melted butter or margarine and ¼ cup chopped nuts together. Firmly press mixture onto the bottom and sides of a greased 8-inch (20 cm) spring-form pan.
2. Chill evaporated milk.
3. Mix together lemon gelatin and unflavored gelatin. Add boiling water and stir until dissolved. Cool.
4. Combine cream cheese and sugar. Mix until smooth and creamy.
5. Stir in apple purée, vanilla and cooled gelatin mixture to the cream cheese and sugar mixture. Chill until mixture begins to thicken.
6. Beat thickened apple-gelatin mixture while slowly adding chilled evaporated milk. Continue to whip until very light and fluffy.
7. Pour into pie crust and sprinkle with remaining ¼ cup chopped nuts. Chill until firm (about five hours)

Serves 8-10.

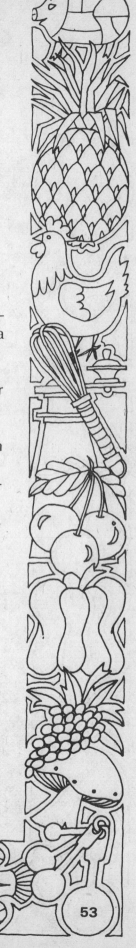

Caramel Crisp Pudding

½ cup sugar
8 tablespoons water
3 oz (90 g) diced white bread
2 eggs
2 cups (500 ml) milk

1. In a small saucepan dissolve the sugar in the 4 tablespoons of water. Rapidly boil until the mixture caramelizes. Cool slightly. Slowly add another 4 tablespoons of water and boil again.
2. Butter an oven-proof dish and put the diced bread into it. Pour the caramel over the bread and allow to soak in.
3. Beat the eggs until light. Heat the milk and pour onto the eggs. Strain the mixture and pour over the bread. Allow to stand for 15 minutes and then bake in a 300°F (150°C) oven for about ½ hour or until the bread is crisp.

Serves 6.

Cream Cheese and Apricot Flan

Pastry:
1 cup flour
pinch of salt
¼ cup (62.5 g) butter
    or margarine
cold water

Filling:
½ lb (250 g) cream cheese

⅓ cup sugar
1 can apricot halves

Glaze:
2 tablespoons red
    currant jam
2 tablespoons water
1 tablespoon lemon juice

1. Sift the flour and salt into a mixing bowl. Rub in butter or margarine with your fingertips until mixture looks like fine bread crumbs. Add enough cold water to form a stiff dough. Chill before rolling out. Roll out to a thickness of ⅛ inch (3 mm). Line the bottom of a flan case and bake in a 450°F (230°C) oven for 15 minutes.
2. Cream the cheese and sugar together. Spread over the bottom of the flan case.
3. Drain the apricot and arrange on the cheese mixture, cut side down.
4. Make the glaze by cooking the jam, water and lemon juice in a small saucepan until dissolved. Then boil briskly until slightly tacky. Pour over the fruit.

Serves 6.

Jam Pudding

2 cups (500 ml) milk
2 tablespoons (40 g) butter
  or margarine
1½ cups fresh bread crumbs
2 tablespoons sugar
grated rind of one lemon
2 eggs, separated
2½ tablespoons sugar
½ cup jam

1. Put butter or margarine in a saucepan with the milk and bring to a boil.
2. Mix bread crumbs, sugar and grated rind and pour hot milk mixture over it. Mix well. Cool.
3. Add beaten egg yolks, blend well and pour into an oven-proof dish. Bake in a 350°F (180°C) oven until set.
4. Beat the egg whites until stiff. Beat in the sugar.
5. Melt the jam in a small saucepan and spread over the top of the baked pudding. Spread the meringue on top and bake in a 300°F (150°C) for about 30 minutes or until the meringue is crisp.

Serves 6.

Fluffy Tapioca Pudding

4 tablespoons (60 g)
  small seed tapioca
pinch of salt
2 cups milk (500 ml)

1½ tablespoons sugar
1 egg, separated
1 teaspoon vanilla

1. Wash the tapioca and soak in enough water to cover for 30 minutes. Drain.
2. Add tapioca to the salt and milk in a saucepan and bring to a boil. Reduce heat and simmer, stirring constantly, until cooked. Cool.
3. Add the sugar mixed with the egg yolk and vanilla.
4. Beat the egg white until stiff and fold into the mixture.
5. Pour into a well-buttered oven-proof dish and bake in a 375°F (190°C) oven for about 20 minutes.

Serves 4-6.

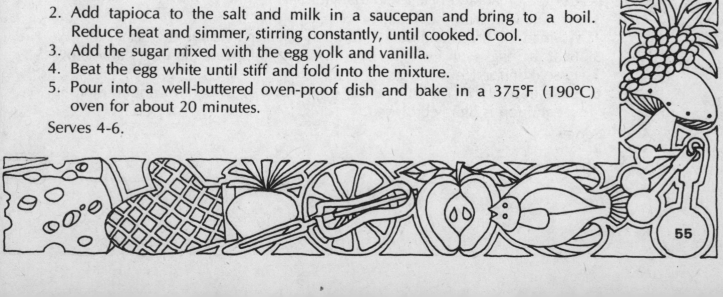

Chocolate Chiffon Pie

Pastry:
1 cup plain flour
pinch of salt
¼ cup (62.5 g) butter
  or margarine
cold water

Filling:
2 oz (60 g) semi-sweet chocolate,
  grated

½ cup (62.5 ml) boiling water
1 tablespoon gelatin
¼ cup (62.5 ml) cold water
3 egg yolks
½ cup sugar
¼ teaspoon vanilla
½ cup sugar
3 egg whites, stiffly beaten
½ cup (125 ml) cream, whipped

1. Sift flour and salt into a mixing bowl. Rub in butter or margarine with your fingertips until mixture looks like fine bread crumbs. Add enough cold water to make a stiff dough. Roll out to a thickness of ⅛ inch (3 mm) and line the bottom of a 9-inch (23 cm) pie tin. Bake in a 450°F (230°C) oven for 15 minutes. Cool.
2. Melt chocolate in boiling water.
3. Soak gelatin in cold water for five minutes. Stir into chocolate mixture until gelatin dissolves.
4. Beat egg yolks with ½ cup sugar until light and fluffy. Add to gelatin mixture. Add salt and vanilla, mix well and cool.
5. Beat ½ cup chocolate mixture and pour into baked pie shell. Chill until firm.
6. Just before serving, spread whipped cream on the top.

Serves 6-8.

Bread and Butter Pudding

8 slices of white bread,
  buttered
2 oz (60 g) dried fruit

2 tablespoons sugar
2 eggs
3 cups (750 ml) milk

1. Butter an oven-proof dish.
2. Cut the bread and butter into triangles.
3. Mix the fruit with the sugar.
4. Arrange the bread and butter, fruit and sugar in layers in the dish.
5. Beat the eggs with the milk. Pour this over the bread and butter and allow to soak in for 15-20 minutes.
6. Bake in a 350°F (180°C) oven for 45 minutes to an hour or until custard is set and top is lightly browned.

Serves 4.

Peach Upside-Down Pudding

2 tablespoons maple or light corn syrup	½ cup sugar
¾ lb (375 g) fresh peaches (or canned peaches), sliced	2 eggs
	½ teaspoon baking powder
	1¼ cups flour
½ cup (125 g) butter or margarine	a little milk

1. Grease a cake tin and put a round of waxed paper on the bottom. Spread golden syrup over the paper and arrange the peach slices over the golden syrup.
2. Cream the butter or margarine and sugar and beat in the eggs.
3. Sift together the baking powder and the flour and stir into the butter and sugar mixture. Add enough milk to give a soft dropping consistency.
4. Spoon the mixture onto the peaches and bake in a 400°F (200°C) oven for 35-40 minutes or until well risen and brown.
5. Turn the pudding upside down and serve warm.

Serves 6.

Rice Pudding

3 tablespoons (45 g)
   short-grain rice
2½ cups (625 ml) milk
2 tablespoons sugar
butter or margarine
grated nutmeg

1. Wash the rice and put into a well-buttered casserole dish with the milk and sugar.
2. Put a few shavings of butter or margarine over the top and sprinkle with grated nutmeg.
3. Bake in a 300°F (150°C) oven for 2-3 hours. During the first hour of cooking, stir a couple of times, then leave undisturbed for the rest of the baking time.

Serves 4-6.

(If desired, raisins may be added before cooking.)

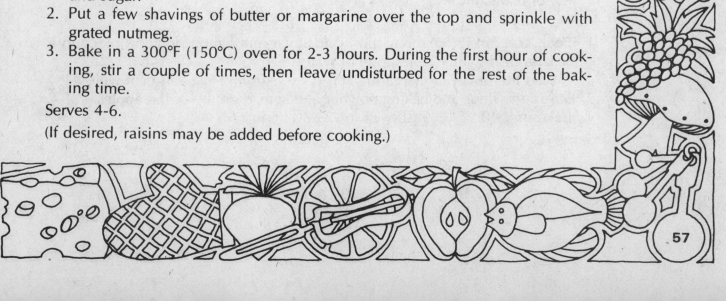

57

Chocolate Pudding

2 oz (60 g) semi-sweet
  chocolate
½ cup (125 ml) milk
2 cups fresh white
  bread crumbs
2 tablespoons (40 g) butter
  or margarine

2 tablespoons sugar
1 egg, separated
1 teaspoon vanilla
¼ teaspoon baking powder
blanched almonds

1. Break the chocolate in small pieces and melt it in the milk. Pour onto the bread crumbs and soak for 15-20 minutes.
2. Cream together the butter or margarine and the sugar until light and fluffy. Beat in the egg yolk, then the soaked crumbs.
3. Add the vanilla and mix well.
4. Beat the egg white until stiff and fold into the chocolate mixture. Finally, fold in the baking powder.
5. Pour into a well-buttered mold and steam gently for one hour or until well risen and firm.
6. Unmold and decorate with blanched almonds.

Serves 6.

Apple Pudding

1 lb (500 g) cooking apples
½ cup sugar
grated rind of one lemon
3 tablespoons (60 g) butter
  or margarine

2 tablespoons sugar
1 egg
½ cup flour
¼ teaspoon baking powder

1. Peel, core and slice the apples. Add sugar and lemon rind and place in a baking dish with 1 tablespoon of water.
2. Cream the butter or margarine and sugar. Add the egg and beat well.
3. Stir in the flour and baking powder and spread on top of the apples.
4. Bake in a 400°F (200°C) oven for 25-30 minutes.

Serves 6.

Yoghurt Dessert

2½ cups sugar
3 cups (750 ml) water
2 teaspoons lemon juice
3 eggs
1 cup sugar
1 cup yoghurt

1 cup sifted flour
1 teaspoon baking powder
1 teaspoon grated lemon peel
1 teaspoon grated orange peel
whipped cream

1. Combine sugar, water and lemon juice in a saucepan. Cook over a low heat, stirring constantly, until sugar is dissolved. Simmer for 15 minutes. Cool. Set aside.
2. Beat eggs with the 1 cup of sugar. Add yoghurt, flour, baking powder and peels. Beat until smooth.
3. Pour into a greased 9-inch (23 cm) square cake tin. Bake at 400°F (200°C) for ½ hour.
4. Before cake has cooled cut into desired number of servings. Pour syrup over the hot cake, cover and let stand until all the syrup is absorbed. Chill.
5. Serve with whipped cream.

Serves 8.

Flamed Apples

6 apples
¼ cup (62.5 g) butter
   or margarine
2 tablespoons brown sugar

2 teaspoons cinnamon
1 tablespoon lemon juice
4 tablespoons brandy
whipped cream

1. Peel and core the apples and cut into ½-inch (10 mm) slices.
2. Melt butter or margarine in a frypan and gently sauté the apple slices for one minute on each side. Sprinkle with brown sugar, cinnamon and lemon juice and continue frying, basting with the syrup until apples are soft. Put on a serving dish.
3. Warm the brandy in a small saucepan. Set alight and pour over the apples.
4. Serve the apples with syrup from the dish and whipped cream.

Serves 6.

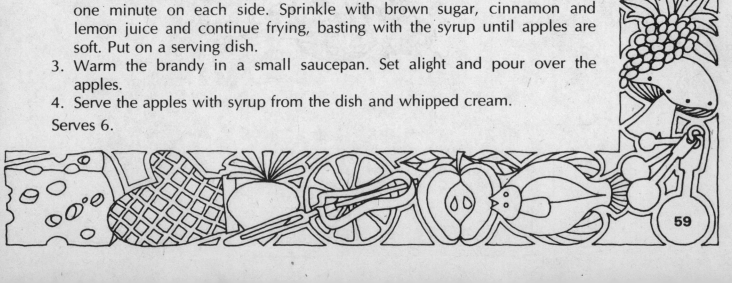

Banana Crisp

> 6 medium bananas,
>   cut in ½ inch (10 mm) slices
> ¼ teaspoon salt
> ½ cup vanilla wafer crumbs
> ¼ cup (62.5 g) butter
>   or margarine
> ⅓ cup brown sugar
> ½ teaspoon cinnamon
> whipped cream

1. Arrange sliced bananas in a buttered casserole. Sprinkle them with salt.
2. Combine vanilla wafer crumbs with the butter or margarine. Add sugar and cinnamon and mix well. Sprinkle over bananas.
3. Bake in a 350°F (180°C) oven for about 20 minutes or until top is browned.
4. Serve warm topped with whipped cream.

Serves 6.

Sautéed Bananas

> bananas (as many as needed)
> flour
> butter or margarine
> sugar
> ice cream

1. Cut bananas in half lengthwise. Cover with flour.
2. Melt butter or margarine in a frypan and sauté the bananas until they are slightly brown. Drain.
3. Arrange on a serving dish and sprinkle with sugar.
4. Serve with ice cream.

Pineapple-Banana Upside Down Cake

½ cup (125 g) butter
  or margarine
¾ cup sugar
1 egg
2 cups flour
2 teaspoons baking powder
½ teaspoon salt

¾ cup (187 ml) milk
1 banana, mashed
⅓ cup (83 g) butter
  or margarine
⅔ cup brown sugar
1 cup crushed pineapple
½ cup chopped nuts

1. Cream butter or margarine and sugar. Add beaten egg and mix well.
2. Sift flour, baking powder and salt. Add gradually with the milk to the butter and sugar mixture.
3. Fold in mashed banana.
4. Melt butter and sprinkle brown sugar on the bottom of a cake tin (8 inches or 20 cm square). Carefully put crushed pineapple and chopped nuts on top.
5. Pour batter over this mixture and bake in a 350°F (180°C) oven for 25-30 minutes.

Serves 6.

Coconut Cream Pudding

1 coconut
4 egg yolks
¾ cup sugar
¼ cup (62.5 ml) water
2 teaspoons lemon juice

1. Drain milk from coconut and grate coconut meat. Cook milk and grated coconut meat in the top of a double boiler for ½ hour. Strain through several thicknesses of cheesecloth.
2. Beat egg yolks and stir in coconut cream.
3. Cook sugar and water together for five minutes. Add slowly to egg yolk and coconut cream mixture, beating constantly. Cook in double boiler over simmering water, stirring constantly, until thickened.
4. Pour into a serving bowl and chill several hours.

Serves 4.

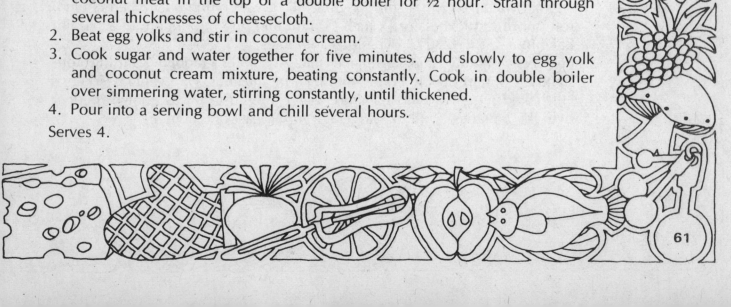

Fried Apple Rings

8 large cooking apples
½ cup (125 g) butter
  or margarine
⅔ cup brown sugar
1 teaspoon cinnamon

1. Core (but do not peel) apples and slice crosswise into half-inch (one cm) slices.
2. Melt butter or margarine in a large frypan. Place the apples in the pan and sprinkle with the sugar mixed with the cinnamon.
3. Cover and cook slowly for 30 minutes or until apples are tender. Baste occasionally but do not turn.

Serves 8.

Banana Cream Pie

Crust:
1 cup flour
pinch of salt
¼ cup (62.5 g) butter
  or margarine
cold water

Filling:
2 cups (500 ml) scalded milk

3 eggs
¼ cup sugar
pinch of salt
½ teaspoon vanilla
2 cups sliced bananas

1. Sift the flour and salt into a mixing bowl. Rub in butter or margarine with your fingertips until mixture is the consistency of fine bread crumbs. Add enough water to form a stiff dough. Chill before rolling out. When chilled, roll out to a thickness of ⅛ inch (3 mm) and line the bottom of a pie tin. Bake in a 450°F (230°C) oven for 15 minutes.
2. Beat eggs slightly, add sugar and salt. Add milk gradually, stirring constantly. Cook in double boiler until mixture thickens. Add vanilla. Cool.
3. Fill baked pie shell with bananas. When the custard has cooled, pour it over the bananas. Chill in refrigerator for at least one hour.

Serves 6.

Baked Apricot Whip

1 lb (500 g) dried apricots
3 egg whites
½ cup sugar
1½ tablespoons lemon juice

1. Put apricots in a saucepan and cover with cold water. Bring to a boil and simmer until tender. Drain. Sieve through a fine strainer.
2. Beat egg whites until stiff. Slowly beat in the sugar.
3. Combine lemon juice and apricots. Gently fold into egg whites.
4. Pour into a buttered casserole dish, put into a pan of hot water and bake for 45 minutes in a 300°F (150°C) oven.

Serves 6.

Nut Pudding

1 egg
¾ cup sugar
2 tablespoons flour
1½ teaspoons baking powder
⅛ teaspoon salt
1½ cups (180 g) chopped nuts
½ cup chopped raw apple
1¼ teaspoons vanilla

1. Beat egg slightly. Add sugar and beat until smooth.
2. Sift flour, baking powder and salt together. Fold into egg and sugar mixture.
3. Add nuts, apple and vanilla and mix well.
4. Pour into a well-buttered 9-inch (23 cm) pie tin.
5. Bake in a 350°F (180°C) oven for 30-35 minutes.

Serves 6.

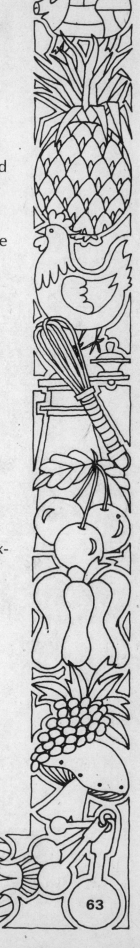

Palatschinken

3 eggs, beaten
1 cup flour
¼ teaspoon baking
   soda
⅛ teaspoon salt
1½ tablespoons sugar
¾ cup (186 ml) milk
sour cream

½ cup sugar
3 egg yolks
2 tablespoons raisins
1 lb (500 g) cottage cheese
⅛ teaspoon salt
3 tablespoons sour cream

Filling:
1½ tablespoons (30 g) butter
   or margarine

1. Mix together the eggs, flour, baking soda, salt, sugar and milk. Beat thoroughly. Make thin pancakes using a well-buttered frypan. Set aside.
2. To make filling, cream together the butter or margarine and sugar. Add the egg yolk and mix well. Add raisins, cottage cheese, salt and sour cream.
3. Spread the filling on each pancake. Roll the pancakes up and place in a well-buttered ovenproof dish. Pour sour cream (thinned with a little milk, if necessary) over the pancakes and heat in a hot oven.

Serves 6-8.

Mocha Float

1 qt. (1 liter) chocolate
   ice cream
6 cups strong coffee
½ cup (125 ml) cream, whipped
cinnamon

Place a scoop of ice cream in a tall glass. Fill with coffee, top with whipped cream and sprinkle with cinnamon.

Serves 6.

Pear Pie

Pastry:
2 cups flour
pinch of salt
½ cup (125 g) butter
  or margarine
cold water

Filling:
⅔ cup sugar

3 tablespoons flour
½ teaspoon nutmeg
½ teaspoon cinnamon
¼ teaspoon salt
5 cups sliced fresh pears,
  peeled
2 teaspoons lemon juice
1 tablespoon (20 g) butter

1. Sift flour and salt into a large mixing bowl. Rub in butter or margarine with your fingertips until mixture looks like fine bread crumbs. Add enough cold water to form a stiff dough. Chill before rolling out.
2. For the filling, combine the sugar, flour, nutmeg, cinnamon and salt. Mix with the pears. Add lemon juice and mix well.
3. Divide the dough in half and roll out to ⅛ inch (3 mm) thick. Line bottom of pie tin. Pour pear mixture into pie tin. Dot with butter. Lay top crust over filling. Seal edges. Cut slits in top of pie to allow steam out during baking. Bake in a 425°F (220°C) oven for 45 minutes.

Serves 6.

Baked Apples

½ cup brown sugar
½ cup (125 ml) water
3 tablespoons (60 g) butter
  or margarine
1 orange, sliced
6 large baking apples,
  peeled and cored

1. Mix together the sugar, water and butter or margarine in a saucepan. Add the orange slices and bring to a boil.
2. Place the apples in a shallow baking dish. Pour the sauce over the top and bake for one hour in a 350°F (180°C) oven. Occasionally baste the apples with the orange sauce.

Serves 6.

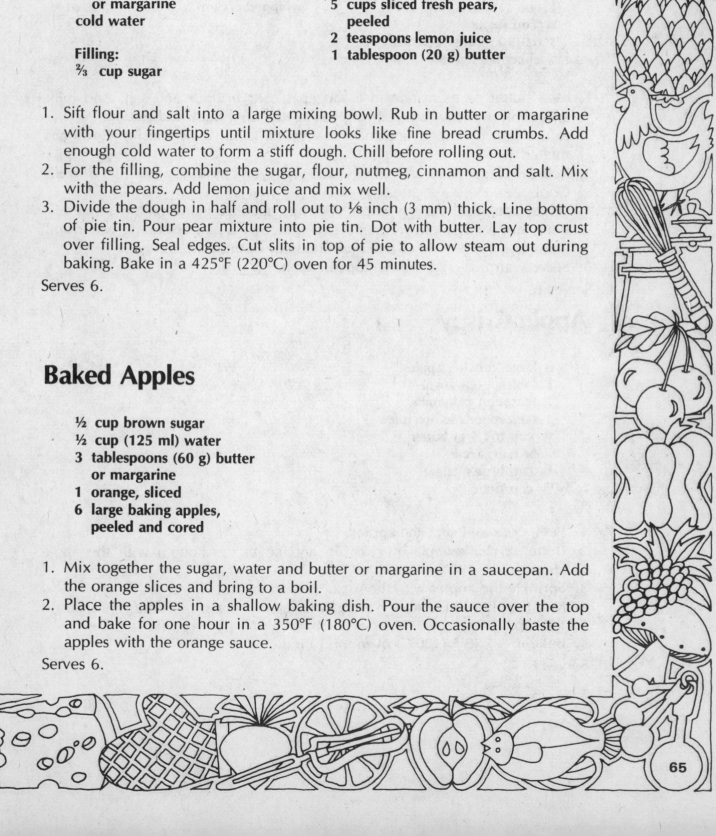

Chocolate Marshmallow Soufflé

3 tablespoons (60 g) butter or margarine	30 marshmallows
3 tablespoons flour	3 egg yolks, beaten
¼ teaspoon salt	1½ teaspoons vanilla
1 cup (250 ml) milk	3 egg whites, stiffly beaten
¼ cup sugar	whipped cream
3 oz (90 g) unsweetened chocolate, grated	

1. Melt butter or margarine in a saucepan. Stir in flour and salt. Add milk and cook over low heat, stirring constantly, until thick and smooth.
2. Add sugar, chocolate and marshmallows and stir until marshmallows are melted.
3. Remove from heat and slowly add egg yolks and vanilla. Blend well. Cool.
4. When cool, fold the egg whites into the chocolate marshmallow mixture.
5. Pour into a casserole or soufflé dish, place in a pan of boiling water and bake in a 350°F (180°C) oven tor one hour or until set.
6. Serve warm or cold with whipped cream.

Serves 6.

Apple Crispy

6 large cooking apples
2 tablespoons sugar
1 teaspoon cinnamon
2 tablespoons lemon juice
¼ cup (62.5 g) butter or margarine
¾ cup brown sugar
½ cup flour

1. Peel, core and slice the apples.
2. Butter a shallow pie or cake tin and cover the bottom with the apple slices.
3. Sprinkle the apples with the sugar, cinnamon and lemon juice.
4. Mix together the butter or margarine, brown sugar and flour. Sprinkle on the top.
5. Bake in a 350°F (180°C) oven for 30 minutes.

Serves 6.

French Apple Slices

Pastry:
2 cups flour
½ teaspoon salt
¾ cup (187 g) butter
   or margarine
2 egg yolks
7 tablespoons cold water
1 tablespoon lemon juice

Filling:
10 large cooking apples
¼ cup sugar
¼ teaspoon salt
1 tablespoon flour
1 teaspoon cinnamon

Glaze:
¾ cup confectioners' sugar, sifted
½ teaspoon vanilla
1 tablespoon water

1. Sift the flour and salt together. Mix in the butter or margarine with a pastry blender or knife until mixture is the consistency of bread crumbs. Add the egg yolks, water and lemon juice and mix until it forms a soft ball. Roll out one half of the pastry and line the bottom of a 7-inch by 12-inch (18 cm by 30 cm) baking dish.
2. Peel, core and slice the apples. Toss lightly in a mixture of the sugar, salt, flour and cinnamon. Place the apples on the pastry.
3. Roll out top crust and place over apples. Cut a few slits in the top crust to allow steam out. Seal edges and bake in a 350°F (180°C) oven for 45-50 minutes. Remove from oven and cool.
4. Mix together the confectioners' sugar, vanilla and water. Spread over the top crust. Cut into squares.

Serves 6.

Bavarian Cream Mold with Strawberries

2 tablespoons gelatin
¼ cup cold water
2½ cups (625 ml) milk
¾ cup sugar
¼ teaspoon salt
1½ teaspoons vanilla
8 macaroons, crumbled
1 cup (250 ml) cream, whipped
fresh strawberries

1. Soak the gelatin in the ¼ cup cold water for five minutes.
2. Scald the milk and add the sugar and salt. Add the softened gelatin and stir until the gelatin is completely dissolved. Chill.
3. When the mixture begins to thicken, add the vanilla and beat until fluffy. Fold in the macaroons and cream.
4. Pour into a ring mold and chill until firm.
5. Unmold and fill center with fresh strawberries.

Serves 6.

Baked Bananas and Blueberries

6 large bananas, peeled
   and cut in half lengthwise
1 cup blueberries
¾ cup brown sugar
1 cup orange juice
2 tablespoons lemon juice
butter or margarine
sour cream (for topping)

1. Put the bananas in a buttered baking dish. Sprinkle blueberries over the bananas and then the brown sugar. Pour orange and lemon juice over all. Dot with butter or margarine.
2. Bake in a 350°F (180°C) oven for 20 minutes. Serve hot, topped with sour cream.

Serves 6.

Blueberry Cottage Cheese Cake

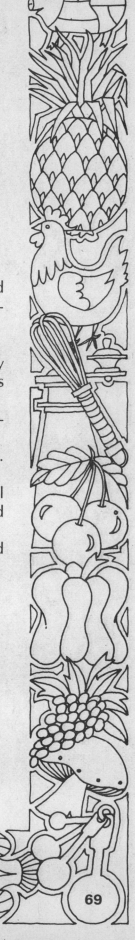

2 tablespoons gelatin
1 cup sugar
¼ teaspoon salt
2 eggs, separated
1 cup (250 ml) milk
1½ cups blueberries
1½ teaspoons grated lemon rind
1½ lb (750 g) cottage cheese
1 tablespoon lemon juice
1 teaspoon vanilla

1 cup (250 ml) cream, whipped
lady fingers (to line 9-inch
   spring form pan)

Topping:
2 tablespoons cornstarch
½ cup sugar
½ cup (125 ml) water
1 cup blueberries
1 teaspoon grated lemon rind

1. Mix the gelatin, sugar and salt together in the top of a double boiler.
2. Beat egg yolks and milk together and add to the gelatin mixture. Blend well. Add the blueberries and cook over boiling water until gelatin is dissolved.
3. Remove from heat. Add lemon rind and cool.
4. Sieve the cottage cheese through a fine strainer and add to the blueberry mixture. Add lemon juice and vanilla and mix well. Chill until mixture is slightly thickened.
5. Beat egg whites until stiff and fold into blueberry mixture. Fold in whipped cream.
6. Line the bottom of a 9-inch (23 cm) spring form pan with the lady fingers. Pour in mixture and chill until firm.
7. To make topping, combine cornstarch and sugar. Add water and mix until smooth. Add blueberries and lemon rind and cook until thickened and clear. Cool.
8. Remove rim from spring form pan, spread topping over the cake and serve.

Serves 10.

Chocolate Soufflé

¼ cup (62.5 g) butter
or margarine
¼ cup flour
½ teaspoon salt
1 cup (250 ml) scalded milk
3 oz (90 g) semi-sweet chocolate,
melted

½ cup sugar
4 egg yolks
1 teaspoon vanilla
4 egg whites, stiffly
beaten

1. Melt the butter or margarine in a large saucepan. Add flour and blend well. Slowly add salt and milk, stirring constantly. Add chocolate and mix well.
2. Add sugar to the egg yolks, then pour into the chocolate sauce, continually beating. Add vanilla.
3. Fold in the stiffly beaten egg whites.
4. Pour into a buttered casserole or soufflé dish which has been sprinkled with sugar. Put in a pan of boiling water and bake for one hour in a 325°F (160°C) oven.

Serves 6.

Fruit Meringue

Meringue:
4 egg whites
¼ teaspoon baking powder
1 cup sugar
1 teaspoon vanilla

Custard:
4 egg yolks
½ cup sugar

2½ tablespoons water
1½ teaspoons vanilla

Topping:
1 cup (250 ml) cream, whipped
1 tablespoon confectioners' sugar
1 teaspoon vanilla
2 cups fresh fruit

1. Beat the egg whites until frothy. Add the baking powder. Beat until stiff. Slowly beat in the sugar. Add vanilla. Pile onto a foil-lined baking tray and bake for one hour in a 300°F (150°C) oven. Cool.
2. For the custard, beat the egg yolks well. Add the sugar and water. Cook in the top of a double boiler over boiling water until it is thick. Cool. Add vanilla and mix well.
3. Topping: Add the vanilla and sugar to the whipped cream. Spread half the mixture over the meringue, then the custard. Cover with the fruit, then with remaining cream. Chill for several hours before serving.

Serves 6-8.

Crêpes with Rum-Nut Filling

1 cup flour
¼ teaspoon salt
2½ tablespoons sugar
½ tablespoon grated
   orange rind
2 eggs
1 cup milk
2 tablespoons (40 g) melted butter
   or margarine

Filling:
1 cup sugar
½ cup (125 g) butter
   or margarine
½ cup chopped walnuts
   (or other nut)
½ cup (125 ml) rum

1. Sift the flour, salt and sugar. Add orange rind.
2. Add slightly beaten eggs and milk to the butter or margarine. Stir into the flour mixture and beat until smooth.
3. Butter a small frypan. When hot, pour in about two tablespoons of batter, tipping the pan so that the batter spreads. When brown, turn and cook other side. Stack until ready to use.
4. To make filling, cream butter or margarine and sugar. Add nuts and rum and mix well.
5. Fill and roll the crêpes. Sprinkle with a little sugar. Warm in a 375°F (190°C) oven before serving.

Serves 6.

Cream Cheese Mold

½ lb (250 g) cream cheese
2 tablespoons cream
¼ teaspoon salt
2 tablespoons lemon juice
1 cup (250 ml) cream, whipped
fresh fruit, cut into
   small pieces

1. Blend the cream cheese with the 2 tablespoons of cream until soft. Stir in the salt and lemon juice.
2. Fold cheese into the whipped cream.
3. Pour mixture in a wet mold and chill until set.
4. Unmold and put fresh fruit on top.

Serves 6.

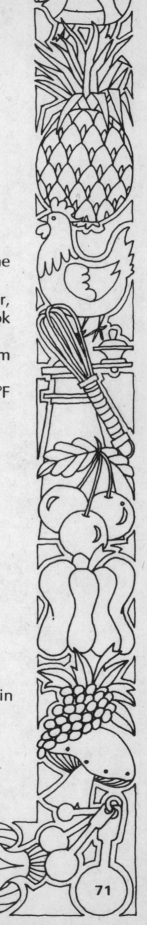

Pineapple Glazed Cheese Pie

Pastry:
1 cup flour
pinch of salt
¼ cup (62.5 g) butter
  or margarine
cold water

Filling:
½ lb (250 g) cream cheese
½ cup sugar
2 tablespoons flour

2 eggs
⅓ (83 ml) cream
1 teaspoon vanilla

Glaze:
½ cup (125 ml) pineapple juice
1 tablespoon cornstarch
1 tablespoon sugar
½ cup crushed pineapple,
  drained
1 teaspoon vanilla

1. Sift the flour and salt into a mixing bowl. Rub in butter or margarine with your fingertips until mixture is the consistency of fine bread crumbs. Add enough water to form a stiff dough. Chill before rolling out. When chilled, roll out to a thickness of ⅛ inch (3 mm) and line the bottom of a pie tin.
2. Cream the cheese until soft. Gradually add the sugar.
3. Stir in flour and whole eggs and mix thoroughly.
4. Add cream and vanilla and mix again. Pour into the unbaked pie shell. Bake in a 350°F (180°C) oven for 40-45 minutes. Cool.
5. For the glaze, cook together the pineapple juice and cornstarch mixed with sugar. Cook until it bubbles. Add crushed pineapple and vanilla and pour over cooled pie. Chill.

Serves 6.

Coconut Ice Cream Balls

2 qt (2 liters) vanilla ice cream
2 cups grated coconut
liqueur of your choice

1. Make ice cream balls using a scoop.
2. Roll in coconut and place in freezer until ready to serve. (Balls hold their shape when individually wrapped in waxed paper.)
3. To serve, place ice cream balls in serving dishes and pour liqueur over the top.

Serves 8-10.

Apricot Pie

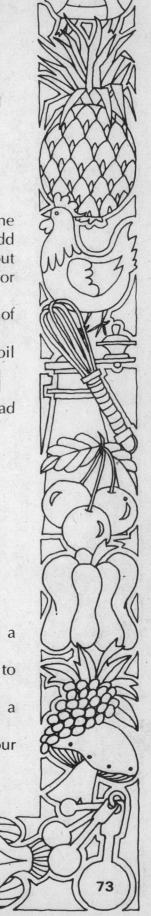

Pastry:
1 cup flour
pinch salt
½ cup (62.5 g) butter
   or margarine
cold water

2 tablespoons sugar
2 tablespoons cream
½ teaspoon vanilla
2 cups puréed apricots
½ cup currant jam

Filling:
3 oz (90 g) cream cheese

1. Sift flour and salt into a large mixing bowl. Rub in butter or margarine with your fingertips until mixture looks like fine bread crumbs. Add enough cold water to form a stiff dough. Chill before rolling out. Roll out to a thickness of ⅛ inch (3 mm). Line the bottom of a pie tin and bake for 15 minutes in a 450°F (230°C) oven.
2. Cream the cheese with the sugar, cream and vanilla. Spread on bottom of cooked pie shell.
3. To purée apricots, put 1½ lb (750 g) of dried apricots in water and boil for a few minutes until tender. Sieve through a fine strainer.
4. Pour the puréed apricots over the cheese mixture.
5. Melt the currant jam in the top of a double boiler. Beat well and spread over the apricots. Chill overnight or for about 8 hours.

Serves 6.

Apricot Mold

1 lb (500 g) dried apricots
½ cup sugar
1½ cups (375 ml) water
1 packet lemon-flavored gelatin
1 packet orange-flavored gelatin

3 cups (750 ml) hot water
½ lb (250 g) cream cheese,
   softened
1 cup crushed pineapples,
   drained

1. Cook apricots and sugar in the 1½ cups water until soft. Sieve through a fine strainer and cool.
2. Dissolve the gelatins in the 3 cups hot water. Let it cool until it begins to thicken.
3. Mix the apricot mixture with the gelatins and pour half this mixture in a ring mold. Chill until set.
4. Combine cream cheese with pineapple and spread over the set jelly. Pour remaining gelatin mixture on top. Chill until very firm.

Serves 6.

Crème Brulée with Pears

  2 cups (500 ml) cream
  8 eggs
  ½ cup sugar
  1 large can pear halves
  ¾ cup brown sugar

1. Scald the cream in the top of a double boiler.
2. Beat the eggs and gradually add the sugar. Beat together thoroughly. Add a pinch of salt.
3. Pour the scalded cream over the egg and sugar mixture and return to the top of the double boiler. Beat with a rotary beater until it is thick. Remove from heat and cool.
4. Pour into a baking dish, put drained pears on top. Before serving, sprinkle with brown sugar and broil for one to two minutes.

Serves 6.

Baked Alaska

  1 qt (1 liter) vanilla
      ice cream
  1 sponge cake
  ¼ teaspoon salt
  4 egg whites
  ½ cup sugar
  1 teaspoon vanilla

1. Spread ice cream on sponge cake and put in freezer until ready to serve.
2. Add salt to egg whites and beat until very stiff. Gradually add the sugar, beating constantly. Fold in vanilla.
3. Remove the cake from the freezer and cover with the meringue. Be sure that the meringue completely covers all the ice cream.
4. Bake for 4-5 minutes in a preheated 475°F (250°C) oven or until meringue is slightly brown.

Serves 6.

Pumpkin Chiffon Pie

Pastry:
1 cup flour
pinch of salt
¼ cup (62.5 g) butter
   or margarine
cold water

Filling:
3 eggs, separated
1 cup sugar

1½ cups cooked and
   puréed pumpkin
½ cup (62.5 ml) milk
½ teaspoon salt
½ teaspoon nutmeg
½ teaspoon ginger
1 teaspoon cinnamon
¼ teaspoon ground cloves
1 tablespoon gelatin
¼ cup water

1. Sift flour and salt into a mixing bowl. Rub in butter or margarine with your fingertips until mixture looks like fine bread crumbs. Add enough cold water to form a stiff dough. Chill before rolling out. Roll out to a thickness of ⅛ inch (3 mm). Line the bottom of a pie tin and bake for 15 minutes or until brown in a 450°F (230°C) oven.
2. Beat egg whites until stiff. Gradually beat in ½ cup sugar until mixture stands in stiff peaks. Chill in refrigerator.
3. Put remaining ½ cup sugar, egg yolks, pumpkin, milk, salt and spices into the top of a double boiler. Beat until well blended. Place over boiling water and cook until mixture thickens, stirring constantly. Remove from heat.
4. Soak the gelatin in ¼ cup water for five minutes. Stir into egg yolk mixture until it dissolves. Cool.
5. When pumpkin mixture begins to thicken, fold in the beaten egg whites. Pour mixture into baked pie shell and chill until set.

Serves 6-8.

Sour Cream Apple Pie

Pastry:
1½ cups flour
¼ teaspoon salt
½ cup (125 g) butter
   or margarine
ice water

¾ cup sugar
1½ teaspoons cinnamon
½ teaspoon nutmeg
2 tablespoons flour
¼ teaspoon salt
⅔ cup (166 ml) sour cream

Filling:
6 cooking apples

1. Sift together flour and salt. Mix in butter with a knife or a pastry blender. Add enough water to make a dough (3-4 tablespoons). Halve and roll out.
2. Peel and core apples. Slice thinly.
3. Add sugar, cinnamon, nutmeg, flour and salt to the apples and mix well.
4. Fill pastry-lined pie tin with the apples. Pour sour cream on top. Put on top crust and press edges together. Prick with a fork. Bake for ten minutes in a 450°F (230°C) oven. Reduce heat to 350°F (180°C) and bake for 40 minutes longer.

Serves 6.

Crème Caramel

½ cup sugar
⅔ cup (166 ml) condensed
   milk
2 cups (500 ml) hot water
3 eggs, slightly beaten
½ teaspoon salt
1 teaspoon vanilla
nutmeg

1. Melt sugar in small saucepan over a low heat. Stir constantly until brown. Pour a little into each custard cup, turning so that the sides are coated. Put aside and let set.
2. Combine milk and hot water. Stir into slightly beaten eggs. Add salt and vanilla.
3. Pour into caramel-lined cups and sprinkle with nutmeg.
4. Place cups in a shallow pan of hot water one inch (2.5 cm) deep. Bake in a 325°F (160°C) for one hour or until a knife inserted in center comes out clean.
5. Allow to stand for 10-15 minutes before unmolding. Serve hot or cold.

Serves 6.

Rum Cream Pie

Crust:
1½ cups chocolate
    cookie crumbs
½ teaspoon cinnamon
⅓ cup (83 g) butter
    or margarine

Filling:
6 eggs yolks

1 cup sugar
1 tablespoon gelatin
½ cup (125 ml) cold water
2 cups cream, whipped
⅓ cup (83 ml) dark rum
¼ cup shaved chocolate

1. Combine all the ingredients for the crust and mix well. Firmly press the mixture on the bottom and sides of a 9-inch (23 cm) spring form pan. Bake for ten minutes in a 375°F (190°C) oven.
2. For the filling, beat the egg yolks until light; add sugar and continue beating.
3. Soak the gelatin in cold water for five minutes in a small saucepan. Put over a low flame and bring to a boil. Pour over the sugar and egg mixture, stirring briskly.
4. Fold in the whipped cream. Add the rum and mix gently. Cool until mixture begins to set.
5. Pour into crumb shell, sprinkle with shaved chocolate and chill for several hours until set.

Serves 6-8.

Peaches in Wine

8 large ripe peaches
¾ cup sugar
⅓ cup (83 ml) water
⅓ cup (83 ml) white wine

1. Peel fruit and leave whole.
2. Combine sugar and water and cook for five minutes.
3. Add wine and peaches and simmer, covered, for ten minutes. Turn peaches often while cooking.
4. Put in a shallow dish, cover with syrup and chill.

Serves 8.

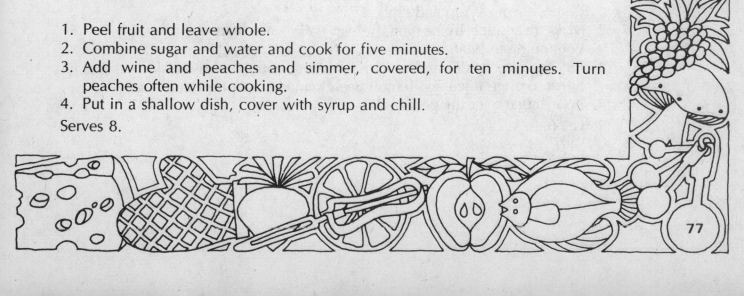

Muesli Ice Cream with Caramel Sauce

    1 qt (1 liter) vanilla ice cream
    1 cup muesli

1. Soften the ice cream slightly.
2. Mix thoroughly with the muesli. Return to freezer until ready to serve.
3. Place scoops of ice cream in a large bowl and serve with Caramel Sauce.

  Caramel Sauce
    1 cup sugar
    ¼ cup cold water
    ½ cup hot water
    one 440 g can condensed milk
    1 teaspoon vanilla
    2 teaspoons light corn
      syrup

Combine sugar and cold water in a saucepan and boil, stirring constantly, until it turns a caramel color. Remove from heat and slowly stir in hot water. Return to heat and cook until mixture is clear. Remove from heat and add condensed milk, vanilla and syrup.

Pears Zabaglione

    2 cups (500 ml) water
    ½ cup sugar
    1 tablespoon grated lemon peel
    1 tablespoon grated orange peel
    1 stick cinnamon
    6 pears, peeled, halved
      and brushed with lemon juice

Sauce:
8 egg yolks
1 cup confectioners' sugar
1 cup orange juice
1 teaspoon grated lemon peel

1. Place water, sugar, peels and cinnamon stick in saucepan and cook until it thickens. Simmer pears in the syrup for ten minutes, turning often. Remove from syrup and chill.
2. Make the sauce by beating the egg yolks until light. Add the sugar while continuing to beat.
3. Put over hot water and continue beating with a wire whisk until foamy. Stir in orange juice and lemon peel. Remove from heat and cool.
4. Pour sauce over the pears.

Serves 6.

Vienna Torte

½ cup (125 g) butter
4 eggs, separated
1 cup sugar
¼ lb (125 g) milk chocolate
1 cup cake flour,
   sifted
¼ cup soft jam

Icing:
¼ lb (125 g) milk chocolate
2 tablespoons butter

1. Using an electric beater, cream the butter. Add the egg yolks, one at a time. Beat well after each addition.
2. Add sugar and beat until light and fluffy.
3. Melt chocolate in the top of a double boiler. Add to the egg mixture and mix well. Add sifted flour. Beat until well blended.
4. Beat the egg white until stiff and gently fold into mixture.
5. Pour into a greased and floured spring-form pan and bake for one hour in a 350°F (180°C) oven.
6. Allow to cool in the pan. When cool place torte, bottom side up, on a serving platter. Spread thin layer of jam over the top.
7. Melt chocolate for icing in the top of a double boiler. Stir in butter. When melted, spread over the jam.

Serves 6.

Apple Compote

8 cooking apples
½ cup sugar
1 cup (250 ml) water
juice of one lemon

1. Peel, core and cut apples into slices.
2. Combine sugar, water and lemon juice in saucepan and boil for five minutes.
3. Add apples and cook slowly until clear.
4. Remove apples and place in serving dish. Boil syrup until it is thick and pour over apples. Cool.

Serves 8.

Chocolate Bottom Pie

Crust:
1½ cups crushed graham
   crackers
4 tablespoons (80 g) butter
   or margarine
4 oz (125 g) sweet chocolate
2 tablespoons hot water

Filling:
3 egg yolks, slightly beaten

½ cup sugar
¾ cup (186 ml) milk
1 tablespoon gelatin
¼ cup cold water
2 tablespoons brandy
3 egg whites, stiffly beaten

Topping:
1 cup (250 ml) cream, whipped
2 tablespoons sugar

1. Mix crackers with melted butter or margarine and press evenly over the bottom and sides of a 9-inch (23 cm) pie dish. Melt chocolate with water, stir and gently pour over the cracker crust.
2. Cook egg yolks, sugar and milk in the top of a double boiler over simmering water until mixture thickens. Remove from heat.
3. Soften gelatin in cold water, place over hot water until dissolved and add to the egg yolk mixture.
4. Cool until mixture begins to set. Add brandy and fold in stiffly beaten egg whites. Pour into chocolate crust. Chill.
5. Just before serving top with whipped cream mixed with sugar.

Serves 6.

Frozen Lemon Custard

2 tablespoons (40 g) butter
   or margarine
3 cups crushed vanilla wafers
3 egg yolks

½ cup sugar
3 tablespoons lemon juice
1 cup (250 ml) cream, whipped
3 egg whites, stiffly beaten

1. Butter a 10-inch (25 cm) square cake tin very well. Line tin with vanilla wafer crumbs, reserving ¼ cup for topping.
2. Beat the egg yolks with the sugar and lemon juice. Add to the whipped cream.
3. Fold in the egg whites and pour into the lined tin.
4. Sprinkle remaining crumbs over the top.
5. Place in freezer overnight or until frozen.

Serves 8.

Strawberry Cheese Pie

Pastry:
1 cup flour
pinch salt
¼ cup (62.5 g) butter
   or margarine
cold water

Filling:
6 oz (185 g) cream cheese

4 tablespoons sour cream
2 pints fresh strawberries
¾ cup (186 ml) water
1 cup sugar
3 tablespoons cornstarch
2 teaspoons lemon juice

1. Make pastry by sifting flour and salt into a large bowl. Rub in butter or margarine with your fingertips until mixture looks like fine bread crumbs. Add enough water to form a stiff dough. Chill. Roll out and cover the bottom of a pie tin. Bake in a 375°F (190°C) oven until golden brown.
2. Cream the cheese and sour cream together and spread over baked pie shell.
3. Wash and hull the strawberries. Place one cup of strawberries in a saucepan with the water and simmer for about five minutes.
4. Combine sugar and cornstarch. Mix with cooked strawberries. Stirring constantly, cook until syrup is clear and thick. Add lemon juice and cool.
5. Place remaining uncooked strawberries in the pie shell on top of the cheese. Pour cooked strawberries and syrup on top. Chill.

Serves 6.

81

Apricot Mousse

    1 large can apricots
    water
    1 packet lemon-flavored gelatin
    1 tablespoon brandy
    1 cup (250 ml) cream, whipped

1. Drain apricots (reserve syrup) and put them through a fine sieve or purée in an electric blender.
2. Add enough water to the syrup to make 1¾ cups (436 ml) of liquid and heat to boiling. Add gelatin and stir until dissolved. Cool.
3. Add puréed apricots and brandy. Place in refrigerator until it is beginning to thicken.
4. Remove from refrigerator and beat slightly with a rotary beater. Fold in whipped cream.
5. Pour into a serving dish and chill until firm.

Serves 6.

Norwegian Torte

2 cups (500 ml) very strong coffee	2 eggs
1 cup sugar	2 cups sifted flour
2 tablespoons cocoa	½ teaspoon baking soda
1 cup raisins, chopped coarsely	2 teaspoons baking powder
½ cup (125 g) butter or margarine	½ teaspoon salt
1 cup sugar	1 teaspoon cinnamon
½ teaspoon vanilla	1½ teaspoons nutmeg
	1 teaspoon ground cloves

1. Combine coffee, one cup sugar, cocoa and raisins in a saucepan. Bring to a boil and simmer for fifteen minutes. Cool.
2. Cream butter or margarine with sugar until light and fluffy. Add vanilla, eggs (one at a time). Beat well.
3. Sift remaining ingredients and add alternately with the coffee mixture.
4. Bake in a greased 10-inch (25 cm) square cake pan in a 350°F (180°C) oven for one hour. Cool.
5. Sprinkle with confectioners' sugar and cut into squares.

Serves 6-8.

Pineapple Torte

Cake:
¼ cup (62.5 g) butter
  or margarine
½ cup sugar
4 egg yolks, well beaten
1 cup cake flour
¼ teaspoon salt
2½ teaspoons baking powder
⅓ cup (83 ml) milk

Meringue:
4 egg whites
¾ cup sugar
1 teaspoon vanilla
¾ cup (90 g) chopped walnuts

Filling:
1½ tablespoons confectioners' sugar
1 cup crushed pineapple, drained
½ teaspoon vanilla
1 cup (250 ml) cream, whipped

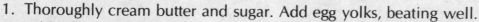

1. Thoroughly cream butter and sugar. Add egg yolks, beating well.
2. Add sifted dry ingredients alternately with the milk. Pour into two 8-inch (20 cm) square cake pans lined with waxed paper. Bake in a 350°F (180°C) oven for 15 minutes.
3. For meringue, beat egg whites until stiff. Add one tablespoon of sugar at a time, beating constantly. Add vanilla. Spread on top of each cake layer and sprinkle with nuts. Return layer to oven and bake for 15 minutes longer. Cool and remove from pans.
4. Mix sugar, pineapple and vanilla with whipped cream.
5. Place one layer of cake, meringue side down on a serving dish. Spread filling over the layer. Put second layer on top, meringue side up.

Serves 6-8.

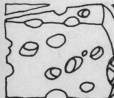

Spiced Prunes

1 lb (500 g) prunes
1 cup (250 ml) vinegar
1 cup sugar
1 cup (250 ml) water
1½ teaspoons ground cloves
1½ teaspoons cinnamon
½ teaspoon salt

1. Rinse prunes. Cover with cold water. Boil for 10 minutes. Drain.
2. Combine vinegar, sugar, water, spices and salt. Boil for one minute.
3. Add prunes and bring to a boil. Cool.
4. Allow to stand overnight in the refrigerator. (One week is even better.)

Serves 6.

Oranges Alaska

8 large oranges
3 egg whites
5 tablespoons sugar
vanilla ice cream

1. Cut off tops of oranges and scoop out pulp being careful not to break the skin of the oranges.
2. Place the orange shell in the freezing compartment of the refrigerator for at least 5 hours.
3. Beat the egg whites until stiff. Continue beating while gradually adding the sugar. Beat until meringue stands in peaks.
4. Chop the oranges segments into small pieces.
5. Half fill the orange shells with the orange segments. Pack in some vanilla ice cream and top with a large scoop of meringue.
6. Place under a very hot broiler until lightly browned. Serve immediately.

Serves 8.

Compote of Fruit

2 cups (500 ml) water
2 cups sugar
10 ripe peaches, peeled
and halved
10 ripe plums, halved

2 lemons, thinly sliced
2 oranges, thinly sliced
½ cup (80 g) whole blanched almonds
½ cup (125 ml) sherry

1. Combine sugar and water in a large saucepan. Boil for five minutes.
2. Add peaches, plums, lemons, oranges and almonds and boil for ten minutes.
3. Add sherry and mix well. Cover and, after it has cooled, place in the refrigerator to chill for several hours.

Serves 6-8.

Peach Kuchen

2 cups flour
¼ teaspoon baking powder
½ teaspoon salt
¼ cup sugar
½ cup (125 g) butter
or margarine

6 large peaches, peeled
and sliced
1 teaspoon cinnamon
2 egg yolks
1 cup (250 g) sour cream

1. Sift flour, baking powder, salt and 2 tablespoons sugar into a bowl. Add butter or margarine and mix until mixtures looks like fine crumbs. Spread into a buttered 20 cm (8-inch) baking pan and press crumbly pastry on bottom and sides.
2. Arrange peach slices over pastry and sprinkle with remaining sugar and cinnamon.
3. Bake for 15 minutes in a 400°F (200°C) oven.
4. Mix together egg yolks and sour cream and pour over peaches. Bake for 30 minutes longer.
5. Serve warm or cold.

Serves 6.

Mocha Torte

6 eggs
1 cup sugar
2 tablespoons instant coffee
1 cup cake flour

Frosting:
2½ cups (625 ml) cream, whipped
3 tablespoons confectioners' sugar
1 teaspoon vanilla
2 teaspoons instant coffee

1. Separate eggs. Beat egg whites until stiff. Continue to beat while gradually adding sugar.
2. Beat egg yolks and fold into egg whites.
3. Sift together flour and coffee and add it, a tablespoon at a time, to the egg mixture.
4. Pour into a well-buttered and floured cake pan and cook in a 325°F (160°C) oven for one hour.
5. Remove from the pan and allow to cool for several hours. Cut into three layers and spread frosting between the layers and on top of the torte.
6. To make frosting, combine whipped cream, icing sugar, vanilla and instant coffee.

Pears in Orange Sauce

6 pears, peeled
1½ cups (375 ml) water
¾ cup sugar
½ cup (125 ml) orange juice
¼ cup (62.5 ml) lemon juice
2 tablespoons orange rind, grated
½ cup (125 ml) sherry
¼ teaspoon cinnamon

1. Combine water, sugar, orange juice, lemon juice and orange rind in a saucepan. Simmer for 5 minutes.
2. Add sherry and cinnamon and cook for two minutes longer.
3. Simmer the pears in the syrup until tender, turning often.
4. Put pears in individual dishes and pour sauce over them. Chill well.

Serves 6.

Chocolate Meringue Pie

4 egg whites
¼ teaspoon baking powder
1 cup sugar

Filling:
6 oz (185 g) semi-sweet chocolate
4 egg yolks
1 teaspoon vanilla
2 egg whites, stiffly beaten
1 cup (250 ml) cream, whipped
shaved chocolate

1. Beat the egg whites until stiff, adding baking powder. Add sugar and continue beating until glossy. Spread into a 10-inch (25 cm) pie plate and bake in a 300°F (150°C) oven for one hour.
2. Place the chocolate into the top of double boiler. Put over hot water and melt the chocolate. Remove from heat.
3. Beat in the yolks and cool.
4. Fold in the egg whites and vanilla.
5. Fold in half the whipped cream and pour into the cooled meringue shell. Spread remaining cream over the top.
6. Sprinkle with shaved chocolate and chill for several hours.

Serves 6.

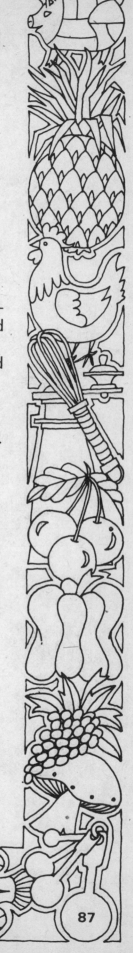

Blender Cheese Pie

Crust:

1½ cups graham crackers, crushed
½ cup (125 g) butter or margarine

Filling:
¾ lb (375 g) cream cheese
2 eggs
2½ tablespoons milk
¼ cup sugar
3 teaspoons vanilla
2 teaspoons lemon juice
1 teaspoon grated lemon rind

Topping:
1 cup (250 g) sour cream
¼ cup sugar
1 teaspoon vanilla

1. Crush the crackers finely. Melt the butter or margarine. Mix together. Line a pie tin with the cracker crumbs and press down very firmly. Set aside.
2. Put cream cheese, eggs, milk, sugar, vanilla, lemon juice and lemon rind in an electric blender and mix for one minute at a medium speed. Pour mixture into the pie shell and bake in a 375°F (190°C) oven for 20-25 minutes. Cool.
3. Combine the sour cream with the sugar and vanilla. Mix well and pour over the cooled cheese pie. Bake for seven minutes in a 475°F (250°C) oven. Cool before serving.

Serves 8.

Strawberry Pancakes

3 egg yolks
¾ cup cottage cheese
¼ teaspoon salt
¼ cup flour
¼ cup (62.5 ml) milk
3 egg whites, stiffly beaten
1 pint fresh strawberries
¼ cup (62.5 ml) water
1 tablespoon cornstarch

1. Beat the egg yolk and the cottage cheese together until smooth.
2. Mix in the salt, flour and milk. Fold in the egg whites.
3. Cook in a buttered 7-inch (18 cm) frypan, using about 2 tablespoons pancake batter. Turn when bubbles begin to break. Cook other side. Set aside.
4. Cut strawberries in half. Mix cornstarch with the water in a saucepan. Stir in strawberries and cook until mixture is clear — about five minutes.
5. Pour strawberry sauce over the pancakes and serve immediately.

Serves 4.

German Apple Pancake

3 tablespoons lemon juice
4 green apples, peeled, sliced very thinly
2 tablespoons (40 g) butter or margarine
6 eggs, beaten
1 teaspoon salt
1 cup (250 ml) milk
1 cup flour
1 tablespoon lemon juice
brown sugar

1. Mix apples with the lemon juice.
2. Melt the butter in a large fry-pan. Sauté the apples for about 5 minutes. Put in a baking dish.
3. In a bowl, add salt and milk to the eggs beating constantly. Pour batter over apples and bake in a very hot oven 450°F (230°C) for 20 minutes. Reduce heat to 350°F (180°C) and bake for 10 minutes more.
4. Sprinkle with lemon juice and brown sugar and serve.

Serves 6.

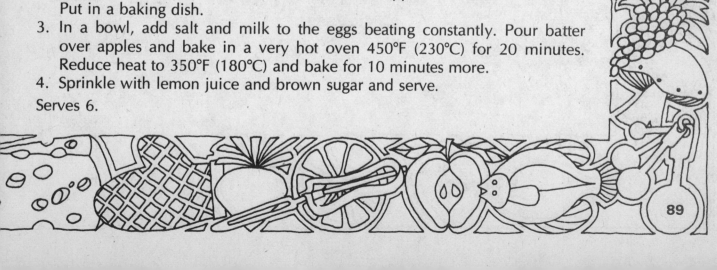

Cheese Torte

2 cups graham crackers,
   crushed
½ cup sugar
1 teaspoon cinnamon
½ cup (125 g) butter or margarine

Filling:
4 eggs
1 cup sugar
⅛ teaspoon salt
juice of one lemon
grated rind of one lemon
1 teaspoon vanilla
1 cup (250 ml) cream
1½ lb (750 g) cottage cheese
¾ cup flour
whole toasted almonds

1. Crush the graham crackers finely and mix with the sugar, cinnamon and melted butter or margarine. Set aside ½ cup of the mixture to sprinkle on top of torte.
2. Butter a 9-inch (23 cm) spring-form pan. Spread the graham cracker mixture on the bottom and sides and press firmly. Set aside.
3. Beat the eggs with the sugar until light. Add salt, lemon juice, grated lemon rind and vanilla and mix well.
4. Stir in the cream and cottage cheese and mix well. Stir in flour.
5. Strain through a fine sieve or purée in an electric blender. Stir until smooth.
6. Pour into cracker-lined spring-form pan. Sprinkle with remaining crumb mixture.
7. Bake in a 325°F (160°C) oven for one hour. Turn off heat and allow to cool in the oven for another hour. Open door for last 30 minutes.
8. Decorate with whole almonds after torte has cooled.

Serves 10.

Pears Cardinal

6 fresh pears
2 cups (500 ml) water
1½ cups sugar
2 teaspoons vanilla
¼ teaspoon salt
Cardinal Sauce

1. Peel the pears.
2. Mix water, sugar, vanilla and salt in a saucepan and bring to a boil.
3. Add whole pears and simmer, turning pears occasionally in syrup, for 20-25 minutes.
4. Cool pears in the syrup. Remove pears.
5. Place pears upright on individual serving plates and spoon sauce over each pear.

Serves 6.

Cardinal Sauce
¾ lb (375 g) strawberry jam
   (or any other red jam)
1 tablespoon lemon juice
1 tablespoon light corn syrup

Combine ingredients and heat in top of a double boiler over hot water, stirring until smooth. Remove from heat and chill in refrigerator.

Fluffy Lemon Pie

Crust:
375 g vanilla wafers
¼ lb (125 g) butter
  or margarine

Filling:
juice of 4 lemons
grated rind of two lemons
1 cup sugar
6 egg yolks
1 tablespoon gelatin
½ cup cold water
6 stiffly beaten egg whites
¾ cup sugar

1. Crush the wafers and combine with the softened butter or margarine. Line the bottom and sides of a 9-inch (23 cm) spring form pan. Set aside.
2. Place the lemon juice, rind and 1 cup sugar in the top of a double boiler. Place over hot water and stir until dissolved. Slowly add the egg yolks.
3. Raise the heat until the water is simmering. Cook egg mixture until it thickens.
4. Soak gelatin in cold water for five minutes. Add to the egg yolk mixture and stir until dissolved. Remove from heat and cool.
5. Gradually beat ¾ cup sugar into stiffly beaten egg whites. Fold into gelatin mixture.
6. Pour into crust-lined spring form pan. Chill for several hours.

Serves 6.

Apricot Strudel

1 cup (250 g) butter
  or margarine
1 cup (250 g) sour cream
1 teaspoon salt
2 cups flour

Filling:
1 lb (500 g) dried apricots
¼ teaspoon powdered cloves
¼ teaspoon cinnamon
¼ cup sugar
1 cup shredded coconut
½ lb (250 g) chopped nuts
½ cup glace cherries, diced
confectioners' sugar

1. Mix the butter or margarine with the sour cream, salt and flour. Chill in the refrigerator overnight.
2. Soak the dried apricots overnight in enough water to cover.
3. Drain the apricots and put through a food mill or chop very finely.
4. Add cloves, cinnamon, sugar, coconut, nuts and cherries and mix well.
5. Roll out the chilled dough ⅛ inch (3 mm) thick. (Roll in a rectangular shape.) Spread the filling over all the dough and roll up (like a jelly roll).
6. Place on a baking tray and bake in a 350°F (180°C) oven for 45 minutes. Sprinkle with confectioners' sugar. When cool, cut in slices and serve.

Serves 6.

Quick Crème Brulée with Pears

1 large can pear halves,
  drained
2 cups (500 g) sour cream
½ cup brown sugar,
  tightly packed

1. Place pears in a shallow baking dish.
2. Spread with sour cream and sprinkle with brown sugar.
3. Put under a broiler about three inches (8 cm) from the heat until sugar caramelizes. Serve hot.

Serves 4-6.

Baked Custard

2½ cups (625 ml) milk
2 eggs
2 tablespoons sugar
nutmeg

1. Heat the milk without boiling it.
2. Beat the eggs with the sugar and pour the milk on, beating well.
3. Strain the mixture into an oven-proof dish or into individual dishes, sprinkle with nutmeg and bake in a 300°F (150°C) oven for about 20-30 minutes or until set.

Serves 6.

Index

Fruit flan 38
Fruit meringue 70

German apple pancake 89
Glazed apple squares 30
Graham cracker torte 18

Honey fruit yoghurt 14

Jam pudding 55

Lemon apple cheese cake 53
Lemon chiffon pie 23
Lemon cream pudding 19
Lemon fluff refrigerator cake 32
Lemon meringue pie 51
Lemon souffle bread pudding 46

Milk coffee jelly 21
Mocha cream pie 45
Mocha float 64
Mocha torte 8
Muesli ice cream with caramel sauce 78

Norwegian torte 82
Nutty cheese cake 33
Nutty pudding 63

Orange Alaska 84
Orange Ambrosia 51
Orange custard 26
Oranges with cream 17

Palatschinken 64
Pavlova 20
Peach cobbler 13
Peach kuchen 85
Peaches in Wine 77
Peaches Riviera 20
Peach upside-down pudding 57
Pears Cardinal 91
Pear compote 24
Pear pie 65
Pears in orange sauce 86
Pears zabaglione 78
Pineapple-banana upside down cake 61
Pineapple cottage cheese cake 31
Pineapple glazed cheese pie 72
Pineapple torte 83
Plum and peach compote 24
Pumpkin chiffon pie 75
Pumpkin pudding 25

Quick crème brulée 94

Raisin cream pie 10
Raisin pudding 17
Raspberry pudding 33
Rhubarb pie 50
Rice pudding 57

Rich cherry torte 11
Rich chocolate pudding with vanilla sauce 16
Rum cream pie 77
Russian cream 50

Sautéed bananas 60
Sour cream apple pie 76
Sour cream sultana pie 49
Spiced prunes 84
Strawberry cheese pie 81
Strawberry cream pie 22
Strawberry pancakes 89
Strawberry whip 40
Strawberry shortcake 42

Vanilla wafer dessert 41
Vienna torte 79

Yoghurt cheese cake 27
Yoghurt dessert 59

ass: 8000 - 5 / S/3